Two
Years

Circulation

By:
icon303

Two Years

To:
Every setback
And fair-weather friend

Two Years

Published by Coyote Blood Press & Paradisiac
Publishing.
No part of this book may be reproduced
Without expressed, written consent or permission
Of the author or publishing entities,
Except for brief quotes for press or review purposes.

Cover Art by icon303

ISBN: 9798713798963

Twitter: @yugo_icon303

IG: @icon303

www.icon303.com

Two Years

Circulation

By:
icon303

Two Years

"Embrace nothing: If you meet the Buddha, kill the Buddha. If you meet your father, kill your father…"

Yugo tripped on a raised piece of concrete protruding over a tree root. Luckily, it was late enough that only police were roaming the streets. He had made it to the glass front door of his "apartment" building; a former hotel, now decaying over a lowly dive bar. The bar recently tried to do his hometown's version of Bar Rescue, but failed quite miserably, as none of the creepy, down-trodden patrons ever went elsewhere. It was hard for someone with any natural instinct to feel comfortable there. The Strathmore Hotel that once housed travelling businessmen in the 50's, houses creeps and weirdos that somehow make the bar's aura soft and angelic; reliable, though, to a desperate 25-year-old man in need of a quick, cheap place to stay. It was such a joke that Yugo snickered every time he slipped his key into the front lock, a key that only let residents enter the building; supposedly, to keep the strange out. August in upstate New York was humid and the air was as heavy as the door Yugo drunkenly tossed open. He bounced inside and let the door slam behind him, instantly regretting that decision. The booming clasp of the latch was sure to invoke the first of several unsupervised asylum survivors to peek his nosey head out of his door that surely hid unknown horrors.

He might've been a bit wild, mischievous, and short fused, but Yugo was calm, collected, with good morality most days. Young and handsome, without good self-esteem; he did well with girls and had no idea what they saw in him. Even staying in this dingy place, he had a constant flow of different flappers looking to escape the boredom of normal guys, but still not settle down. One of them, the week or two prior, had told Yugo that a scary, red-haired, man came out in the hall in his underwear; asking her about who she was and why she was there. Yugo apologized profusely and promised he'd take care of it the next time he'd see him.

Walking up the first few stairs, he was praying to whatever deity would listen that this man stayed in his room. He'd noticed him a few times peeking out of his room but could only make out coke bottle glasses and beady eyes watching him walk to his room in the late hours of the night after closing the newly opened bar where he worked. The owners were a wise-assed couple from NYC that would frequently put the main bartenders through trials by fire and made them drink until they couldn't stand any more alcohol, send them home right before 5AM, and expect them back to repeat it the same morning at 9AM. This particular whiskey-laden night, Stephanie, the physically and financially rich Brazilian gaffer from California, was spinning her way through his mind; the message of this fuck face potentially scaring her away infuriating him further than the already seemingly malevolent modus operandi of this, now tangible, but still figurative, John Wayne Gacy.

A few more steps until he reached the second floor of the building, but first floor of the Strathmore, and possibly Gacy's face. His gaze was fixed on the stairs, so he didn't fall and could only see the ceiling lights in his upper peripheral. Yugo tried so hard to not look up, but he knew he had to. He slowly panned upward against his blood pressure demanding he didn't. Maybe, if he didn't make eye contact, he wouldn't have to scare the Ronald McDonald reject. First, just carpet and the second set of stairs entered his vision. Then, the bare feet... He paused, then and there, knowing what was presumably next. Yugo's eyes jumped straight up to rip the band aid off and wasn't as surprised as he'd expected.

A man, well into his 40's, balding on top with long, curly ginger hair fluffed around the sides and back. He was void of color, except for bright rosy cheeks under his thick prescription of glasses, and huge red shirt. Other than that, the only color that existed anywhere near this man was the red hair covering his gluttonous thighs, and Whitey Tighties with a faint yellow tinge to them. Upon the instant confrontation with home-boy, Yugo's adrenaline kicked in and his blood pressure skyrocketed. With his blood being doused in Powers, it made his need to protect every girl that ever came to visit him in that hellhole boil up.

Yugo pointed his vision straight into his eyes as he drunkenly blurted out, "What the fuck do you want?".

The man almost jumped when he heard his tone and stammered out, "Wh- wh- who are you?", shaking on the last word.

"I fucking live here, man. Who the fuck are you? And, why the fuck are you stopping people in the goddamn hallway at this hour, mother fucker? Is this South Africa? Do you like Nazi's? Go to fuckin' bed!" As Yugo said that he gestured towards the man's room and noticed a video game on and paused, some laundry, and soda bottles. "This guy was definitely a chronic masturbator," Yugo thought to himself. The man huddled backward toward his safe place, away from the dodge ball Yugo became. Yugo started up the next flight upstairs to his, and the third-floor corridor of rooms.

He could feel the man's eyes still on him and shouted "Go! Close your fuckin' door and mind your own fuckin' business! I don't want to hear shit you have to say. Put some fucking pants on the next time you try to talk to me, you fucking deviant!"

The man promptly closed his door loudly without slamming it as Yugo ascended; relieved and a bit guilty to be out of that situation.

He hiked the rest of the oak stained stairs and entered through his creaking door, being quiet to try and not wake the old, silent man that lived through the adjoining door. Much like modern hotels, some rooms have the door that allows you to go through, room to room. Yugo wondered if the old man heard any of his sexual exploits, or maybe smelled the ganja. He was never sure, and the man never uttered a word. Once in a while you could hear him cough, but nothing more.

Yugo dove into the nearest notebook he had. Tonight made his mind up and he would write about every tear in reality for the next two years. And, in that, keep and spread the lessons learned. He was in for a journey through the most important faucets life has to offer. Stumbling, falling, running, through pain, love, and freedom, and how each one's full appreciation can't be reached without full comprehension of the adjoining two.

This is the jump.

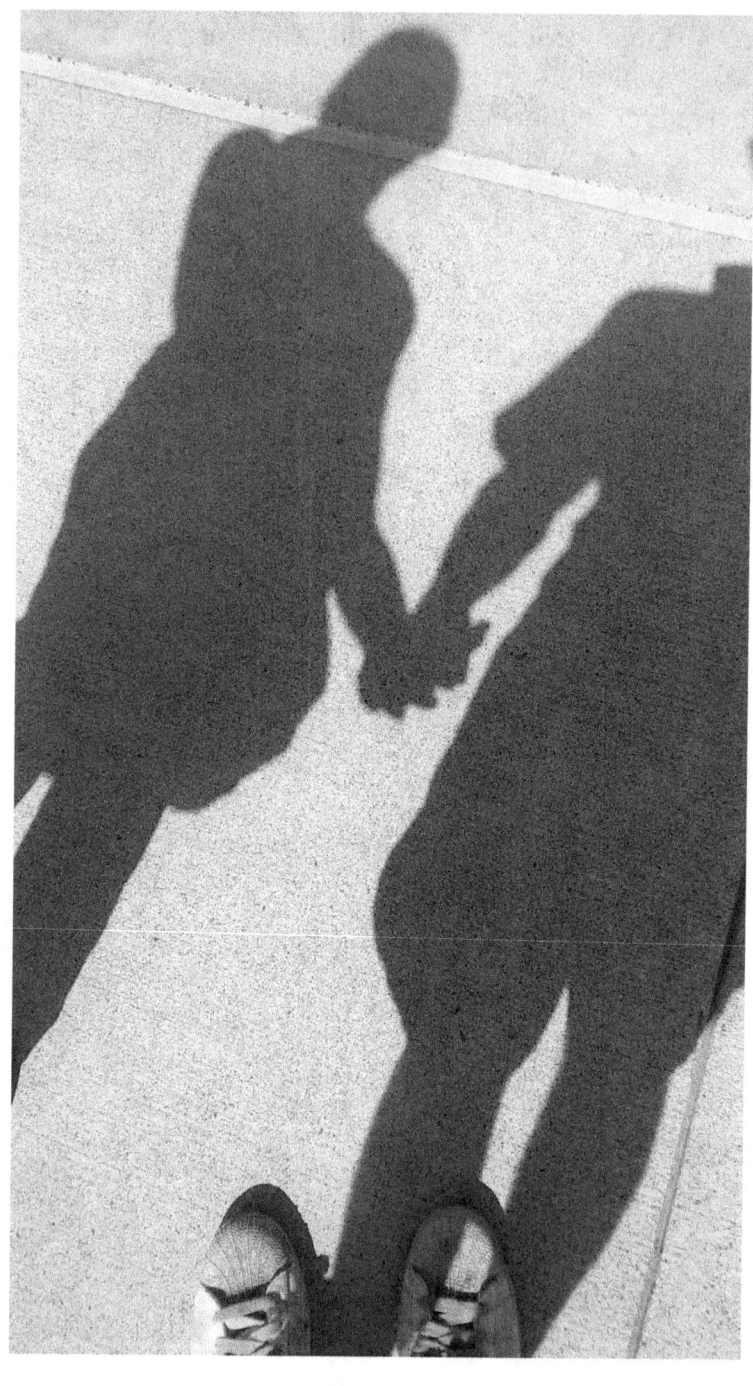

<u>Altruism</u>

With all the sun outside,

I thought of you today.

Whilst I got greens and other things,

I pedaled against the wind.

I knew both were going to be tiring.

And the harder the day got,

It seemed the sun had felt it.

I wanted to text you today

And tell you how much I hated you.

I figured a bridge would be better.

I bet you never thought when you woke up

You would have to talk the sun down.

But along came a Yugo.

Taking what were seemingly my last drags,

I think about how fast I'll fall,

And where I'll hit.

With never having a single concern

For the left or right,

It's no mystery

The only direction I'm looking is down.

Being up here,

I closed my eyes.

Hearing the screams and jeers

 To jump or get down,

Made me think back to past times.

The night I punched a hole in the wall.

The morning I couldn't remember your name.

The afternoon I walked out.

And it made me open my eyes.

I can see police lights coming.

I can see the wind pulling the rain.

I can see the rain falling.

I can see the river overflowing with pain.

Pedaling opposite the wind's decision

Was only making me stronger,

A life without you

Is, seemingly, more like heaven.

I'm only stronger without you.

Without the wind,

The rain would never be directed.

Without rain,

The river would never be full.

Without the river,

There would never be life.

Without you,

I would never know this sorrow.

Without this sorrow,

I would never be this free.

Without being this free,

I could never truly love.

As soon as you pressed send

The future hit me like a fastball to the face.

Downing me,

With my eyes turning into faucets

Of bountiful blood inking my memories.

It reminded me I was going to replay

That moment for years to come.

That storm lasted for 3 days.

Wu Tang tattoos,

Lucid and likely,

I got down a changed man.

Having lived an urchinistic,

Shiny, black, mysterious life,

With spiny hedonistic edges;

Full lessons of things

Better looked at than touched.

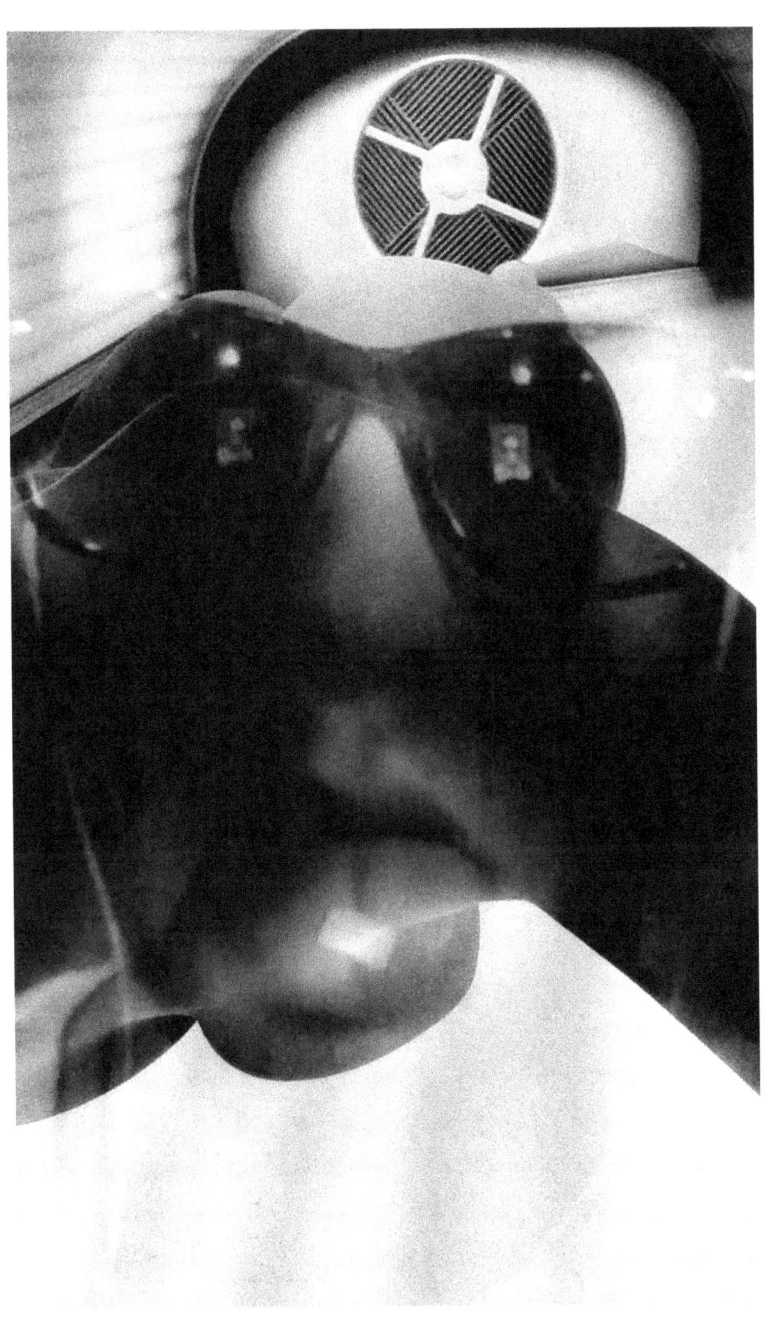

"'Where did you meet?'
He pressed on.
I shrugged and considered a little
rephrasing.
 'I was out for a run.'
'From who?'
I leaned back to take a long, very long,
slow sip of that

beer.**"**
– Dannika Dark

Water Rings

Our entire experience floundered

Like the last customer to stumble out of the bar,

Where the memory of your presence

Gets wiped down.

The half empty glassware

Of your company gets dumped

And washed for reuse.

Water rings remind me it all comes back around.

As you tell me my land of living is paranoid,

I say, "It's just the past's precaution."

One better to have and never need,

Rather need and never have any of.

<u>Secrets</u>

Moving on

Doesn't mean

You forget.

It means

You continue

Living life

And love

Those who

Love you.

The Cure

You're the cure and I'm the sickness.

So, it's no secret that not only

Were we made for each other,

But our love would also lead

To the eventual demise of both

Our previous selves.

You,

Fashionably invented in room

Drained in white walls

With the brightest spectrum of light rays.

And I, as the affectionate virus

Only someone as depraved

As Mr. Levchenko could be,

Lay dormant in the blood stream and vein deltas

Of this world.

That's only as crazy

As your imagination will allow,

Until the perfect antiviral solution

In the 5-foot 7 structure

Of a blond,

With multicolor eyes,

Was injected and crash-landed.

Ground zero was close to home,

Right around the elbow from the dark shadows

I'm accustomed to;

One heart throb from my doorstep.

As you elegantly strolled

Into my field of vision

I already felt weaker

And magnetized to you.

Our hands touched as I left you

Some way to find a cell

To bring you back to me;

As blood brought me

In a scenic circulatory route home,

The very thoughts of where we were both

Going to, from, and where

We were both currently at,

Individually,

Started to gain a black vignette.

By morning,

Life left us no choice

But to have one life,

Almost mechanical and masterful in design,

Yet tragic and ruptured in derivation.

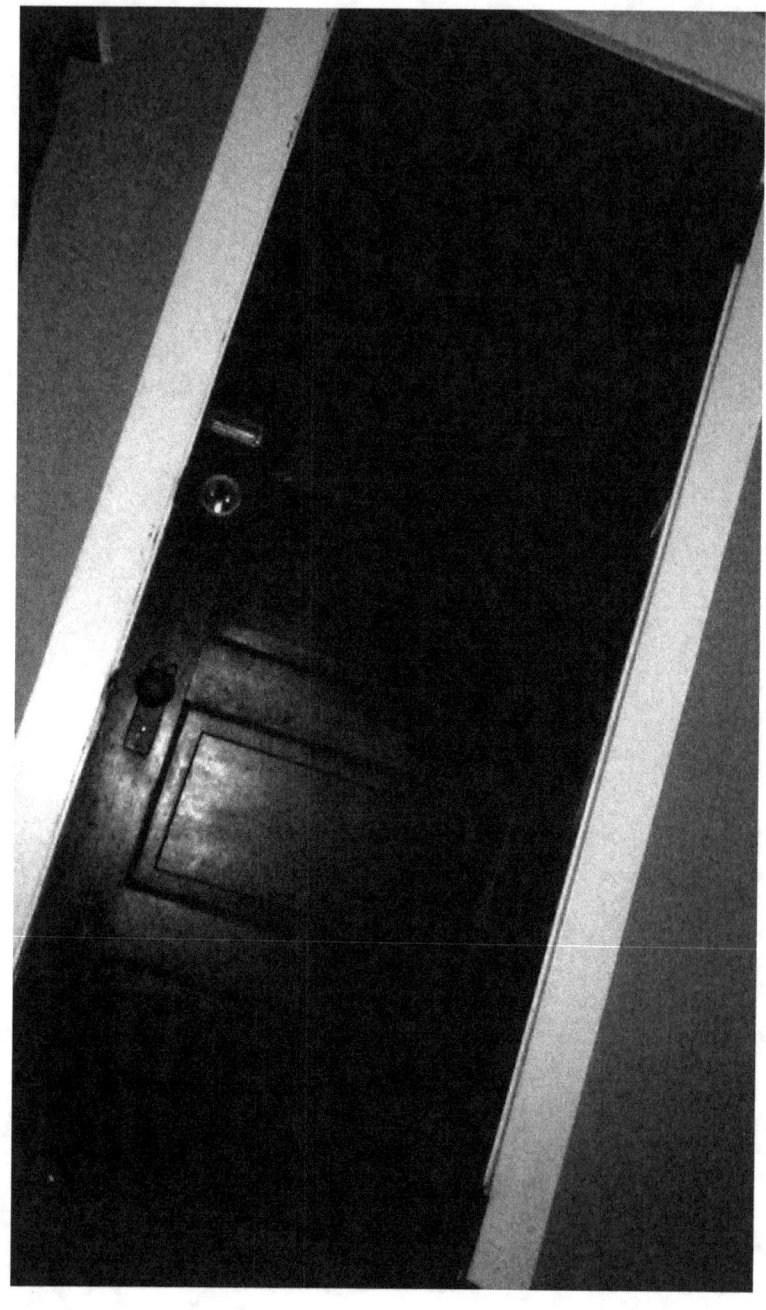

<u>Alice</u>

'Tis hard for a mad hatter,

In a room of Cheshire smiles.

Even worse is the glowing matter

Stretching itself for miles.

Like a clock that's gotten sadder,

Time has forgotten style.

Most of this stuff doesn't matter

Just added mass for the pile.

Consuming some of the latter,

I pondered how worth-while.

And, in blooming free clatter,

Existence has never been so vile.

Prism

That face,
Looking in,
Outside the window
Was scary enough at 4 AM.

I can feel the cold breeze
That face inspired.
A cold, numbing breeze,
That made the leaves tremble.

I sat here,
Staring back.
Frozen against every bit
Of wind hugging my shirtless body.

I don't remember
How it got there,
Outside.

Come to think of it,

I can't recall how long, either.

Smoke lofts in the light of my phone,

Surely lighting my face.

Although in a cloud,

Clearly visible

Was the tension.

As is the wonder

In both our eyes.

That face

Staring at my face,

Outside.

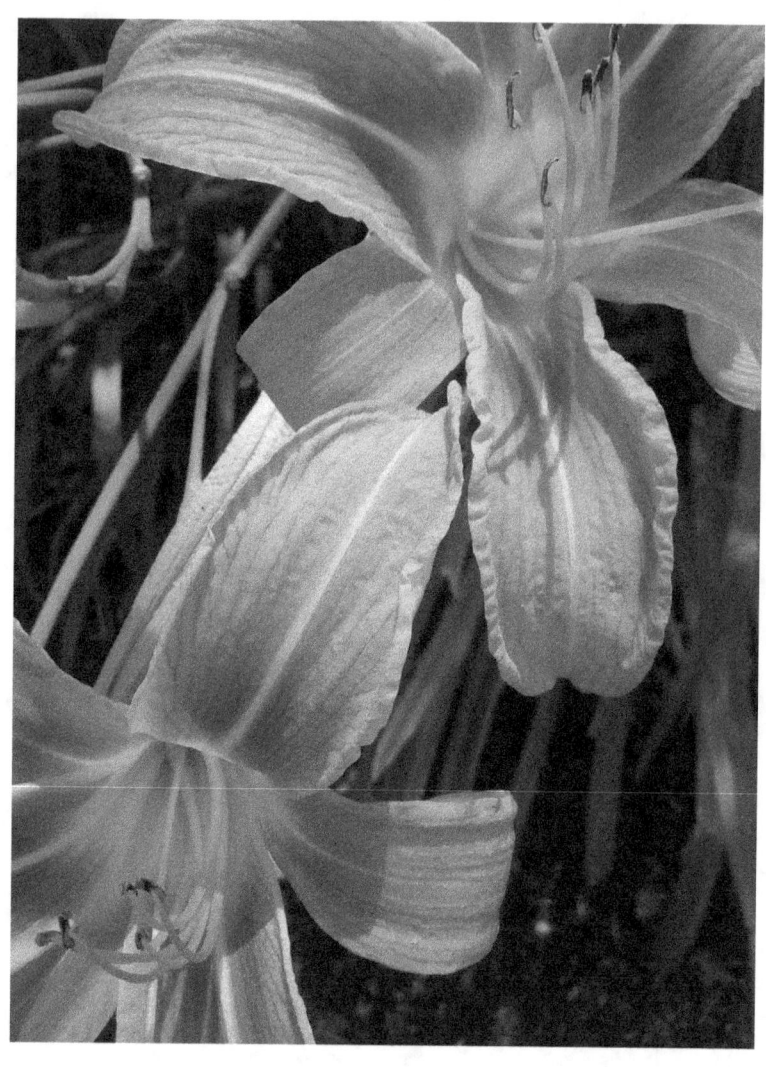

November Remembrance

Winter has swept in a blanket of cold loneliness.

A cold blanket reminiscent of lying in your arms;

Distant and yet attached,

Holding on for your own prosperity.

Clinging and drawing

Like a member of the leech species,

With succubus mechanics and inner workings.

A cold blanket that devours your electric life force

Down to a mere hot day field buzz;

So low no one will know where it's coming from.

Because, surely no one can survive

That minor a vibration.

Using a sort of magnetic vampirism

To grow and add to its own quilted patterns

Of previous bridges burned out

With stripes of dancing contrasts;

Where you as a blanket were supposed to be

Safe and warm,

Flashed to dangerous frost

And memories tainted of the times

I built my own shelter and cozy heat.

Snuggled up to my own fire

And became a blanket on to myself.

With you there was no fuel to continue,

But without you,

I would never have all this.

Leaf Poem Part 1

There are times in life

When you meet someone,

And you see more than what they look like.

More than another leaf

Skating down the sidewalk in August,

Skipping about,

Careless and living to the fullest.

You see,

Instantly,

What the leaf used to be.

You see the leaf's

Original colors and shapes,

And it being a vital,

Life breathing gift to, and of, nature.

And upon seeing the leaf

In its glorious freedom,

Instantly,

You wish you could skate with it.

Be a leaf with it.

Butterflies and Dandelions

I saw you today,
In a field already expired.

Your petals bright in color and bud full in bloom;
So gorgeous, and uniquely yellow,
In that field of cold greens.

I thought of Osho and letting you die there, alone.

Growing old,
Turning into a ball of little parachutes of life;
Giving back to the world the love
You so desperately sought
And never found.
Growing weak;
Creaking as the wind abused you,
And brittle like the world made you feel.

Instead,

I wanted you to feel warmth

One last time.

I picked you and smelled you;

Held you and told you

How beautiful you were

Until every last petal fell.

Was I wrong

For killing the suffering

You were soon to endure?

Was it wrong

To keep you gorgeous forever

In the peripheral memory

Of every person to have passed you by

Without a second glance?

Or should I have

Let you wilt,

Ending like every other forgettable flower?

The beauty in you

Inspired a change in me.

Like the smallest flap

Of the butterfly's wing,

You caused a typhoon.

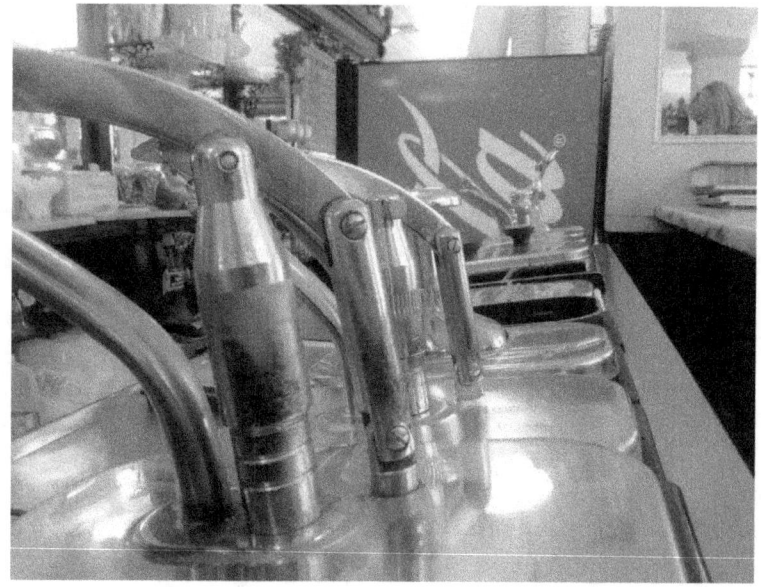

How I Say "Goodnight"

"You already know the answer.
NO."

"Which is about as rude as
Waking up my girl and me at this hour."

"Even if you need advice,
You're drunk and won't remember."

"I'm in bed."

"As unreal as it is, I care about her more."

"Even if you're happy for me,
It doesn't excuse me
For being a dick of a friend."

<u>Shake</u>

I should've said goodbye sooner.

Should've stayed in the woods,

Treating these wounds.

It's less infectious,

But still so lonely.

The entire time I've been here

Feels like this wound will never heal.

Instead, I must suffer

With each, and every, diseased gangrene cell

This city can muster.

Instead, I spend my time picking at it;

Keeping it alive,

When I should let a hand full of maggots

Eat every bit of your rotten pieces of flesh.

Devour your entire stench

And continue healing.

I may be sacrificing all I am

By doing that, though.

For you all would eat me alive, burp,

And forget to even say grace.

This place gives me the chills

Every time I go outside now;

With no meat left on these bones,

It's hard to find warmth.

Even in an embrace.

Instead, I tremble like coconut wind chimes

During a hurricane,

Shake like a baby's death rattle;

Feel the pain few could properly convey.

The ones that figured it out

Left.

And I'm not mad at them for it.

<u>Orion</u>

Oh, life...

It's interesting the tests you give.

You get blessed

With the brightest star one night,

And get woken up by the supernova

Of life's previous mistake the next day.

How do you tell the past to stay still

So that you can have a future?

Or, is it a different perspective?

Is this newly formed mass of carbon

A test to see if you meant

The depression you pained through

For two years, as the eternal summer

Imploded before you and left you in darkness?

Forward movement is the only true

Motion of ambition;

Everything else is selfishly trying

To re-acquire more blessings

Of the past and present.

I want to go back.

There's a place where girls twirl fire

And the moon waves back,

Ever so slightly.

It's like the warmth in the field

Full of random "ha's".

And with that,

I feel comfortable here.

I feel belonged.

Even though my mind has varicosed,

That smile we gave you

For the first time

Will change the plots of the future.

<u>New Lessons Learned</u>

Freedom from the mind

And security of the heart

Is what we innately desire.

Kindness PSA

Ever since you left,

Every day is like Christmas morning.

Every experience is a gift

With a pretty bow and shiny wrapping paper,

Screaming to be let out of a box.

There's always a new person, conversation,

A new sort of event in your life.

Go at it with the same

Intensity and enthusiasm of a child,

Ripping into his new Tonka truck.

Go at it like someone handed you all 5

Teenage Mutant Ninja Turtle movies At once.

Smile,

Be thankful,

And love the people you surround yourself with.

They were once in shiny wrapping paper, too.

Be their bow.

Road Music

I've fallen in love a million times
And no one will ever believe it.

Coming home every night
To a different woman
Already naked and in bed,
Waiting for you seems like a wet dream.

But most will never know
How lonely it is never being alone,
And no one ever knowing the real you.

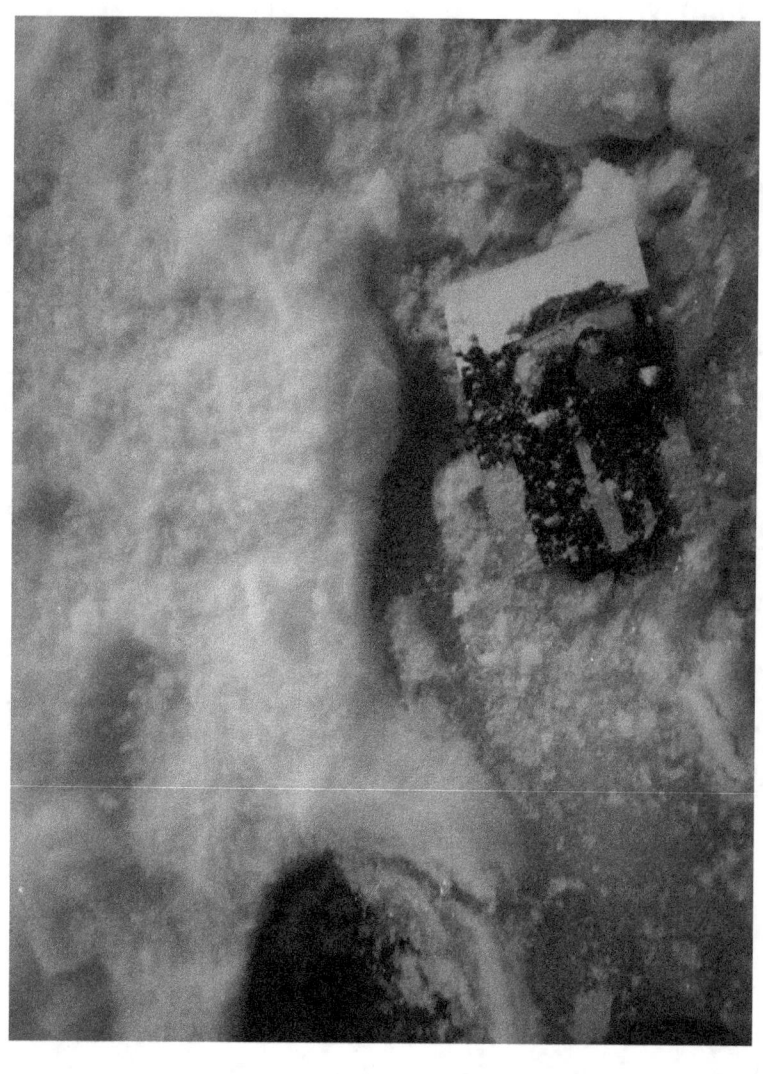

She's Too Much Like Me

Leaning in,

I think my mind must be playing tricks on me again.

Fuck it, though.

Even if it is,

What is life without cliffs to jump off,

Or planes to jump out?

I woke to the sun and tapestry fighting with the wind.

I think the psychedelic flashes

Made me dream of police.

With that in mind,

I immediately awoke.

As soon as my eyes broke,

I noticed a beast sneezed in her safety cove.

The gusts made something tumble on the floor.

What was it?

I disregarded it and moved about.

The beast was soon a foot behind.

I needed a drink after the last few days,
And was almost glad there were no drinking glasses;
Or any other evidence from the weekend.
No glasses.
No trash.
No empty packs of cancer.
No plastic bags, And no trouble.

And when the text came,
I had just placed my last two and a half hits
On my tongue.
"Shit!" I thought,
"Beast-mode probably needs nutrients
And growth hormones."
I scrounged up every scrap that was around.
She hopped and chirped as I walked into the cave,
And noticed the item she must've inhaled.

The answer to today's riddle,
And the beginning of a new one,

Was staring me in the face ever since I woke up.

Coated in Friday's bad decisions,

Beast horded for herself a plastic bag.

No other garbage anywhere.

No mess.

No dismay.

No anything. Just an empty bag of badness

The Beast thought was gold.

Is That You?

Is that you...?
Through the fog and the fuss...?

Only the devil knocks at the door at 3AM,
And my only open eye sees through the nonsense.

But those strings you pull
Cover me like a 'We're All Mad Here' blanket.

And since it's comfortable to me,
I'm sure the madness hasn't stopped.

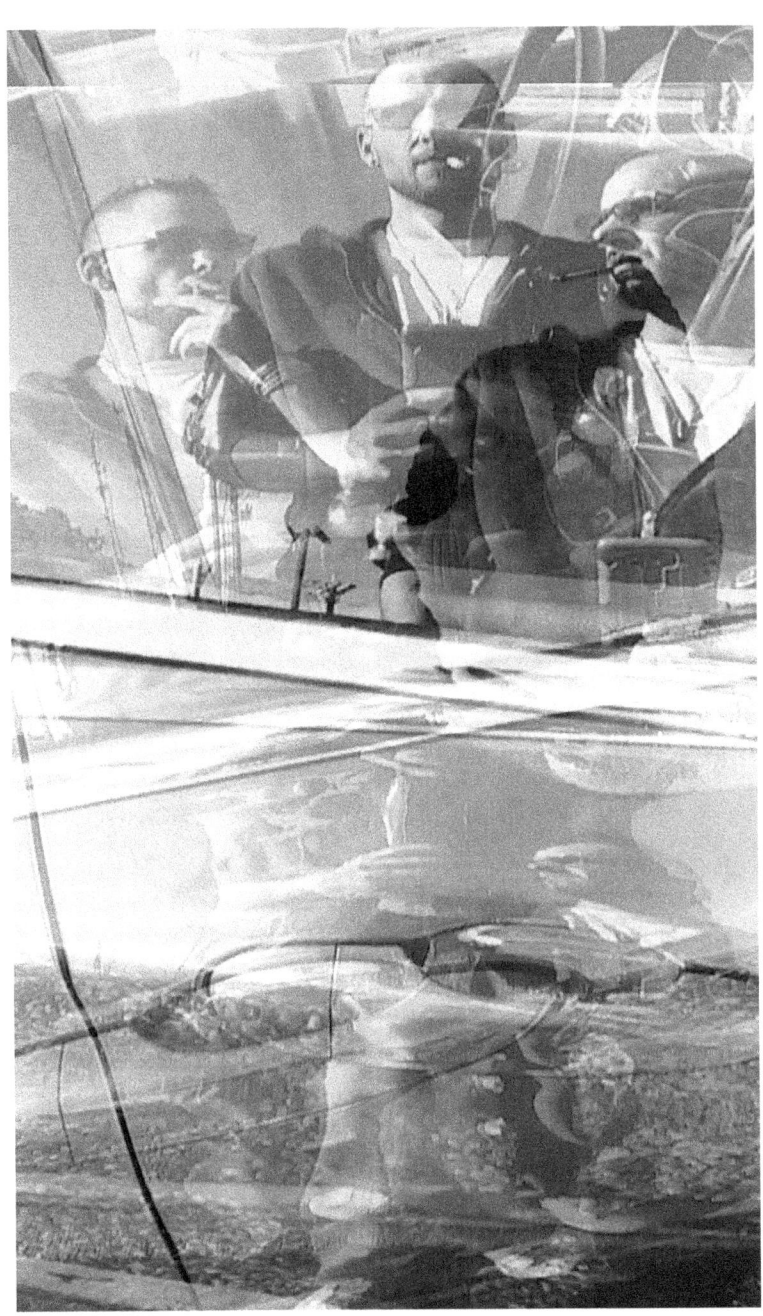

Hilltop Views

Sunset to sunrise,
And back again,
His love for her
Welled up inside,
Forever.

He watched as she chased everything
That made her happy,
Puking and panicking.
No matter the storm,
She loved it.
And whatever that was
Didn't love her back.

So, she was stuck
In wanting what
She couldn't have;
Constantly trying

For "it's" attention,

Until she withered one night

During a pretty sunset.

And as he sat there

The following sunrise,

As still as the cement

He stood on,

It hit him.

He watched like

The sidewalk watched

Everyone walk all over it.

Every sunset

He needed a shower,

To wash away the feeling

Of scuff marks

Her DC's left on his ego.

He loved her so much

That watching killed him inside.

Watching her grow vibrant

As "it" came to the room.

Lighting up like the sun

Reflecting off mirrors
In Egyptian basements;
Making him equally as burnt
As she was beaming.
Only to fizzle
Just as quickly.

Knowing all she needed
Was "its" love.
Not his love.
No, not his love.
Not good enough
To soar with her,
And not good enough
To mend those old scars.

So, he's been stuck there,
Wanting what he can't have.
Constantly trying to tell himself,
"Someone will want me,"
Sunrise to sunset.

God's Eye View

When I look at you,

I see the entire cinematic masterpiece

Of all your smiles and cries;

All the happiness and pain.

I see the random comedies

Your gorgeous mind

Tells to your soul

As you walk about so free.

I see the drama life served you

On a plate of stress and unknown

And all the times you spent alone...

I want, and hope, to see you happy

As the music begins and credits roll.

Exactly!

It makes me want to throw shit.

Not like objects,
But, like actually shit.
Everywhere.

The walls...
The windows...
The merchandise...

Just everywhere.

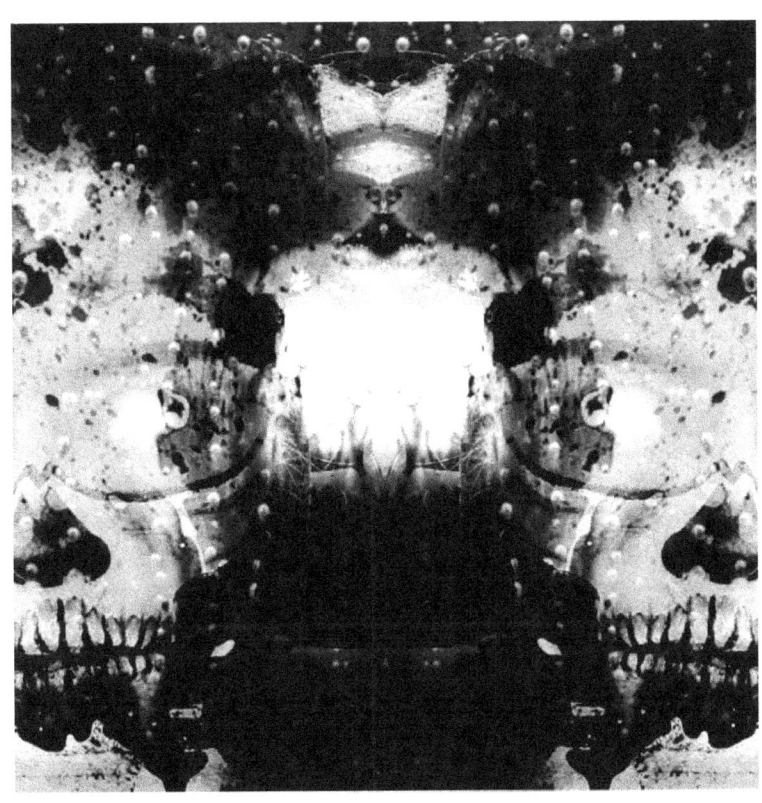

Everything I Love

There were three pieces of ash to be spread.
One in Sydney, Australia,
The other two in Killigrew, Ireland.

The three to never combine but each was related.
Three never seen as traveling had to be reinstated.
Hopes crashed and pulled
From this shore over seeing it all,
Almost cyclostyle in fashion.

Radiant waves and gravity from a small moon
Might not be able to move this heavy earth
Being held on the Sun's spoon.
But, sure as traction,
Those small waves move cities and rations.

More paradoxical than pity;
That ash lingers adjacent to scenes

On movie screens quite well acted,

Dormant yet screaming.

That shore inched back but stayed resilient.

Large stones people threw

Keeping the sands in place.

But soon at any pace will there be wars.

And that shore will be,

Swallowed and forgotten into nevermore.

Joint Glances

Sitting with Mary,

Rolling up,

I glanced around and met your stare.

As I licked the papers,

I thought about what our adhesive could bare.

You smelled so sweet

In between these silk white sheets.

Like the fire at the end of it,

Our beginning burnt from nights to weeks.

So smooth I never coughed once.

For months I loved you intensely.

Every instance left me in depth with you,

We we're in it so much.

Watching our souls touch,

I forgot to get to know you.

Taking another puff,

The cloud was unable to see through.

Coughing at your lines,

Knowing I've heard it before

And they were all deceitful.

The citrus and coffee musk

Turned to smoked fruit and skunk.

From love to lust.

From flush to bust,

And likewise, with us.

Never thought once

You'd be the one I trust.

Now the high from the first time

Is all I'm after.

I couldn't bear the here-after

Or fake anymore laughter.

The Tide

I've always had the pleasure of starting as the pauper.

The lowest.

The tramp,

Who got the kiss from the lady in a turn coat.

The shell on the beach,

Beauty masked by the many.

In most eyes the struggle is

To find something more than pity,

More than a loathing sorrow.

The struggle is the beauty, though.

The work it took to get that kiss,

The unique circumstances that put the coral color

Of your spiraled shell

Directly in a ray of light,

That glimmered for all to see.

In that,

Lives legends.

In that,

King for a day could never describe.

But that was when fur lined hoods made you popular.

That was before.

Before anything bad happened

And you lost trust for everyone,

Worst of all, me.

I wouldn't trust me, either.

When I could've been there to protect you,

Like I promised.

And now when I reach,

You run.

Even though the worst I ever did to you,

Was leave years ago,

You still haunt me.

Now the pauper sits,

Wishing back to that one day as king.

Back to when I was your haven.

Back to the beach.

Even now in the dark,

Rays of light reflect off you,

And you still illuminate my cave.

I think of the waves of our lives crashing together.

Every struggle bringing us closer,

Even though we never saw it.

We will always think about water

Washing away the footsteps in the sand,

But never the underlying grains forever impacted.

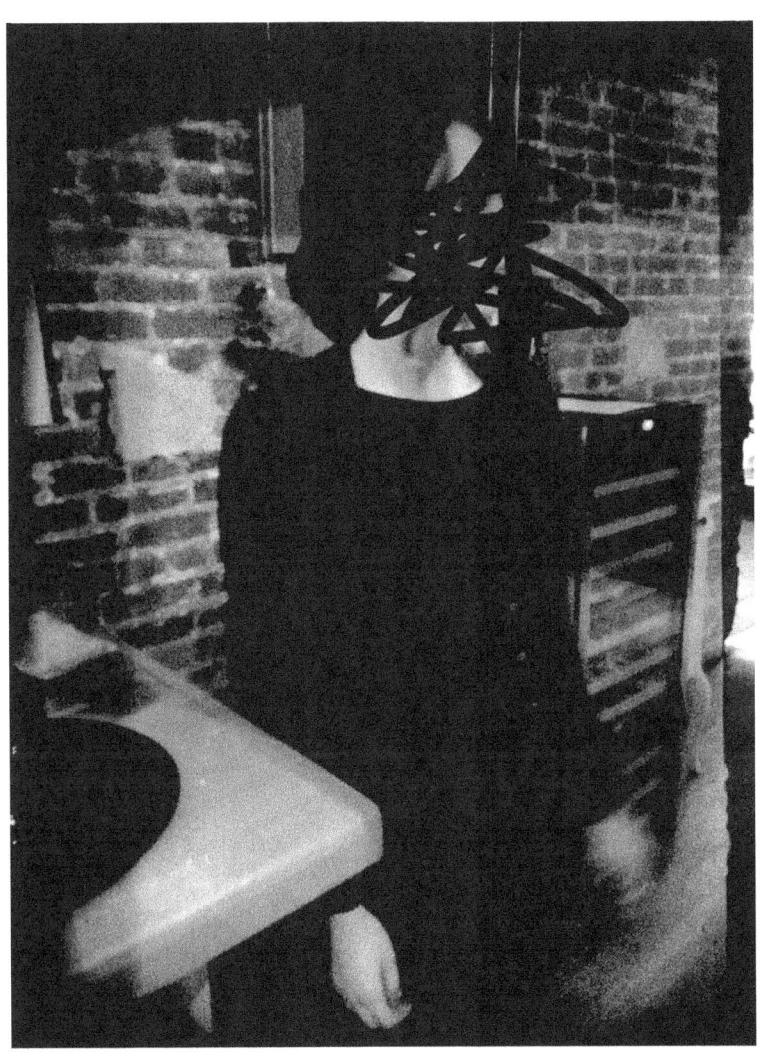

Nixon

The night was littered with
Shouts of, "Get away from my dick!"
And scolds to, "Stop sniffing her panties!"
As the beast that roamed this small
2-bedroom apartment
And tried to figure out the animalistic sounds
That just conspired on the other side
Of the faux-oak doors.

Crashing and claps could be heard in a block,
Or two, radius.
Luckily no police showed,
And I didn't have to clean
The various mysterious illicits;
Eliciting some form of truth.

My brain too fucked to pay any attention
To proclivity or rationale;

Especially with you leaving dawn side.

Not much can change now,

Only sheets in the wind.

Sail that worry, love,

And stow the vests.

I don't want to come out unscathed.

__Due__

The devil knocked again at 3AM
And I didn't know how to answer.
Even with the door closed and dead bolt locked,
I could hear your hooves and laughter.
Your eyes a beaming,
Seemingly drooling,
With light powered hatred
And nails clicking like forks
When a feast is fully plated.
I froze in fear and loathingly peered
Through the peephole at your furious congregation.
Only corrugated opinions correlate to your minions
Who only stop to extrapolate your millions.
It's crazy to expect no scars in the floor
When the heat flows opposite the ceiling
And you're feeling safety no more.
I'm just a beast without horns.
Come hold me now.

Grains in Wood

It's funny now to look back at how
Our fun was all lessons,
And the lessons became fun.

Living a life of freedom
And thinking for myself has me living
Like stinky meat in the streets
Where all you devils had come from.

Accepting the raping offers,
I bend over to the edge
And gaze into your banking lungs.
Grabbing ahold of the grasped bags
Full of money and lag the exhalation
That most of my actions are
Too courageous to be done.

You're scared, yet I'll be running

Whichever way the ocean tugs.

I wasn't even trying but life isn't dying,

Like the end of the morning sun.

We could've had the evening.

All I ask is to believe me.

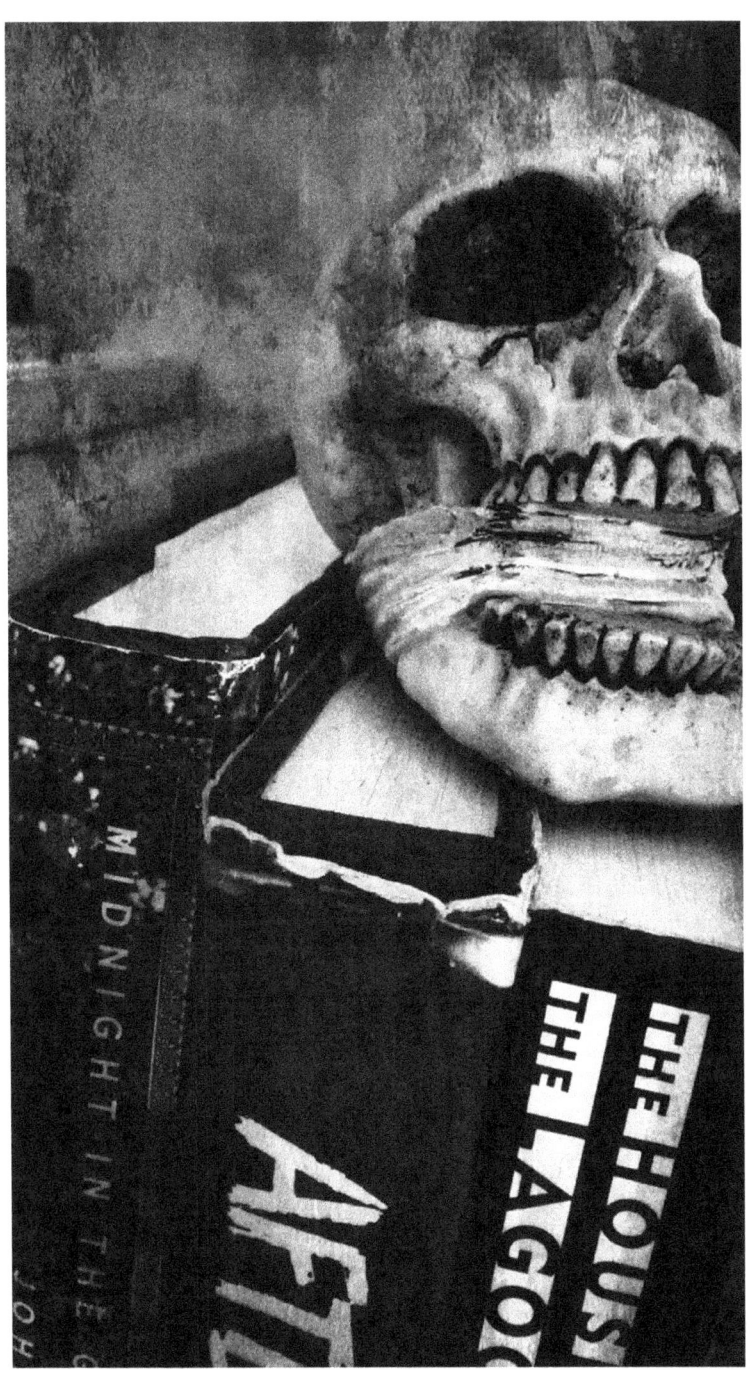

*"**R**eality doesn't impress me.*
I only believe in intoxication,
In ecstasy,
And when ordinary life shackles me,
I escape one way or another.

No more walls. "

–Anaïs Nin

The Bench

The pond glimmered today
As I sat down on warm concrete.
Sun flickered off the wind's paint brush,
Making one last grand firework exhibit for you.
Just you.

Now, that you're with everyone else I love,
Are you lonely?
Did that last day at the pond make you forget all of us?

Or can you see me hugging my dog for comfort?

I talked to your best friend today.
He still thinks you sat at the pond, though,
So you didn't make a mess of the house.
But I can see what you saw.
And you lived it like you were never going
To see it again.

Silently confident on tomorrow's territory,

I'll miss you something ill...

Table Round with Whiskey

In this land of the dreamers,

I pray to have someone fall for me

Half as fast as I do for them.

I can't look into your eyes without wishing

I had a parachute.

Fuck it.

I won't need it.

And, as I leap,

I can almost guarantee

You won't be there to catch me.

Swindled by the look on your face...

The fire, that almost burns

Inside your eyes, told me I'd be OK.

I need an escape.

An escape I found in you;

Soiled by my Brutus.

But I can't let go,

Even when I don't want to hang on any longer.

As if stitched by the scent of your skin,

The feeling of the silk

God made of your skin, glides over me;

Your love was sheets fit for a king,

With the many shiny adornments.

That's why.

That's why I do let this love's death rattle

Heave and crackle

Like a wounded prey running from its hunter;

And from Hell,

It will burn this house to Hades with it.

Now, I'm just praying I'm asleep when it does.

Because some days it's hard

To not combust when all I want is you.

I can feel you reel in,

Then cast back out.

And like a fish about to bite the lure,

I'm just as confused as you when I see it jerked away.

The hunger that wanted to love you every second

Took an immediate left to mistrust.

I hope somewhere parallel
Your hands are wrapped in mine,
Instead of this whiskey in my hands at this table round.

Every time I think of you now,
I picture the slowly decaying flower
Sitting in my freezer
And how much it looks like my liver.
You're no different a chemical as any other drug.
Meaning that it doesn't matter
The intake,
Or inhibitor,
The high is all I want to feel.

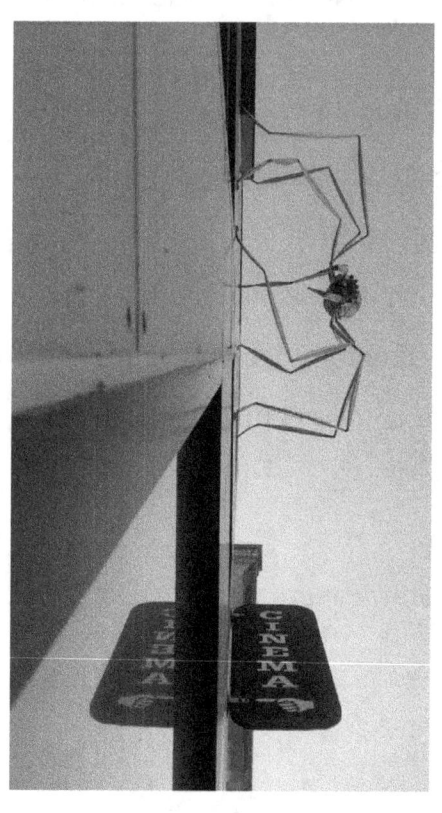

Probable Propaganda

Time is only relevant
To our lifespans.

Snuffleupagus

My father called today.

He said my mother wants to know where I am.

But that's the estrangement.

That's the life.

I'm on the fast route

To health problems,

But I still feel like the Snuffleupagus

Has always snored.

So, tell her I'm going down

To meet the estrangers,

To get a sense of what's right.

Much like most my other decisions,

I know it'll piss her off.

 A woman scorned hath no wrath

Like a son shunned

And forgotten.

Dissent

Imagine a world with dissent and desertion.

Shouldn't be hard,

You're a dreamer.

Seemingly, teamwork is to endure;

Meant to hurt me.

I never meant to hurt them.

I'm an addict when

There's only one thing certain,

My high has become a burden.

Certainly, I never meant for my fears transferred.

But, none-the-less, we're both waking up deterred.

Time for our intelligence to shine;

Wave goodbye.

See you at another time.

Letters to Andy

What's up, Andy?

How are you?

I know we don't know each other,

But you know someone I do.

You guys both were members

Of a purple shield together.

He's my uncle and I've known him forever.

I was wondering,

Since you've been there longer,

If you could do me a favor.

Even though you're superman,

In my eyes,

My uncle was stronger.

So, if you say no,

I'll completely understand,

But he's one of the people

Who taught me to be a man.

Anyways, next time you cross him down the hall,

Tell him I miss him first-of-all.

Tell him this next move is for the pain I'm feeling

As you uppercut his jaw.

Tell him I'm mad as fuck

As you pick him back up.

And, tell him I love him so much.

Tell him I don't let anyone see me cry,

And I wait till I'm alone.

Tell him, come by.

And if this is too much, Andy,

Please let me know.

I just don't know where else to go.

I don't know who else to ask.

How else can I tell him these things

Besides talking to the bottom of my flask?

I haven't had a good month, Andy,

And it'd be great if he stopped in.

Unless he can't see his own doings

And is only seeing my sins....

Regardless, he needs to know I need him.

And, I hope he knows I cared.

I would've came to see him

And tried my hardest to be there.

I want to feel like he's heard me

Or it's hell to pay when I get there.

I'm not a kid anymore; I'm a fucking beast.

I could go on forever,

But I'll let you enjoy the rest of your night...

I'll talk to you guys later.

I'm going back to life,

And it's really depressing

That you both can't come.

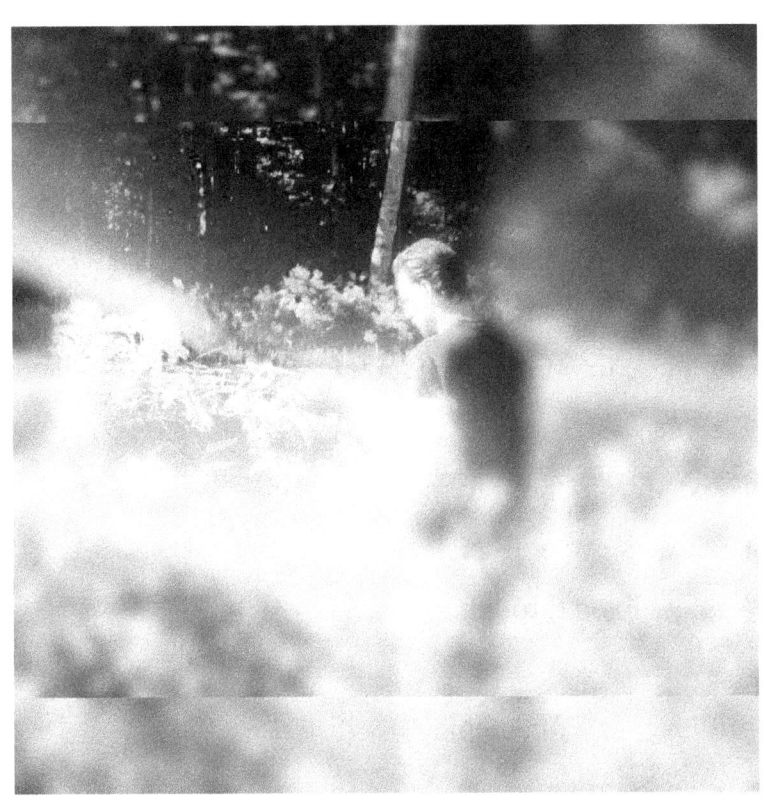

3AM Market Street

Another group of people
Standing by a car I'd rather not see.
They're lost.

Holding onto yesterday's glory,
While missing the most important days,
One more important than today by far;
Tomorrow.
Too damn stubborn to recognize
Their own cycle of mistakes
Already lived through.

But *I'm* crazy for keeping my distance.
It's not common place.
Bar stools are up and crazy looks
Dance across slowed faces as I reply,
"I'm going home."
I'm going home.

Which isn't this place.

Not this ground. Not this texture.

Mines a bit more 3D than most, for sure,

Because the only time

I've ever felt at home

Is when I'm not at home.

Drowned

I wish I made you feel like the first time we met.
I wish there wasn't such a thing as tolerance,
And I could still get as drunk
On every drop of your acid,
Like it was the first time.
Then all the negative things we do
Wouldn't build like brick walls
Our hands punch every time
We're just reaching for each other.

I've been trying to make my heart explode
For 24 months now,
And sober from you for 6.
That alone is thought plasma.
So how can you say you love me,
When you can't understand my own self destruction
And how completely necessary it is?
I'm a bastard born without rhyme or reason.

Secondly, how can I love you?

My closest guess is I deserve nothing more.
Much like Atlantis was overwhelmed,
Probably for karmatic reasons,
I'm 10,000 leagues under the sea.

Still True

Extremities and dangers
Have a way of
Making you lose your path.
Entangled in my own sins,
I lost my escape.

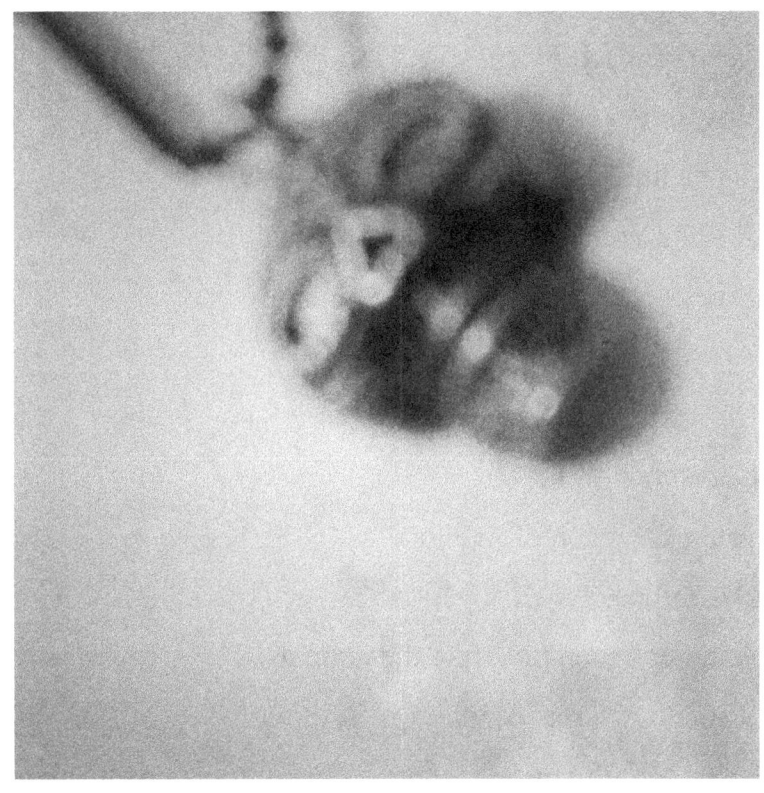

Enslaved

We,

The purposefully enslaved,

Vow our ever-living love,

And admiration, to the overseer,

A.K.A. Your

Faceless voting booth of our future.

Our own greed,

Corruption of power,

And perversion of freedom

Has left us,

And our generation, like the animals;

With no real reason why we do things.

Instead, we're driven by our preprogrammed instincts.

We have children as teenagers

Living crazier and more fast-paced lives,

With no sense of remorse

Or consequence,

As if they're trying to pack as much life,

And experience,

Into the shortest amount of time.

Much like anything fuzzy or feathered,

When Mother Nature wants to flex her strength,

Flying and scampering To the safest places possible.

Usually, to the highest ground.

And with this some important lessons are learned.

When morals and the love of others

Is outweighed by the love of one's own life,

We will slowly tear each other apart

'Til there's nothing left.

And not only will we do this,

But we will take the high road

Singing narcissistic phrases like Y.O.L.O.

The only thing to stop it

Is a collective evolution of the conscious.

And, when these things are happening,

Albeit, through instincts,

It tells us our subconscious

Knows the only thing left to do

Is regard selfish amusement as a diet,

Because our end is inevitable.

If Our Fathers Were the Models

I seem to remember
A morning like grapefruits covered in sugar.
An extra bowl of sugar
To dip all the strawberries.
Sweet smells of cherry Swishers
And stained cups of wine and tea.

It faded.
Every happy moment but those.

A couch with my blankies
And bowl of Cocoa Pebbles.
Quiet laughter and Saturday cartoons,
Waiting for the beast to awaken.

I learned,
Too easily, how life can change.

And like a cold breeze in summer,

I felt the season shift

Every time the beast inhaled.

And like the heat

I felt drained before it began.

And, as I grew,

My shell hardened quickly.

Still on the couch

With my bowl of cereal

Watching cartoons.

Trying desperately to reminisce,

And come to a place

Where I can forgive you.

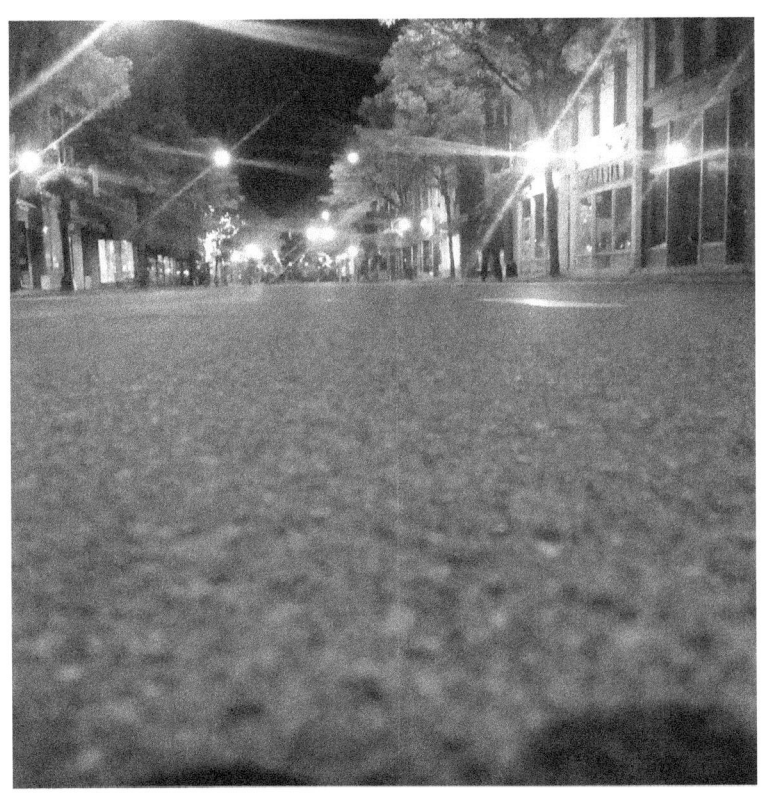

Eventually

Our deaths are not only a decision,
But the processing of how long we want to suffer;
Adversely, how long we'd like those lives we touched
To take to forget us
And move on to the next host.

Adversely, because, it seems to me
That the shorter your life and quicker your demise,
The longer you're missed,
Instead of living long enough
For everyone to anxiously pray for
Eternal sleep on your behalf.

I-86

Seeing you pull away
Like red lights fixed on the tail of a car,
Left I slumped on the shoulder.

Feels like a burning lust that simmers 'til
I'm forgotten.
I loved it, immensely,
The more pain drained inward.

Bouquets

Tangled webs, tangled webs,

Thank God I can see ahead

And watch you spin this web

With an abdomen full of dread..

I feel used and confused,

Instead of the love we fed.

I leaked.

I bled.

Then, went to bed

Like reasonably scouted prowess

On the weekends.

Just as a spark in the dark

Shot across the furthest part

Of the cosmos' spread,

I reached in and found the end.

I gripped and pulled loose,

This dangerous noose,

Like the bride set to wed,

But forever fled.

<u>Mirrored Warning</u>

If you find me depressed,

It's just because I know I can be more.

To you.

To the world.

To me.

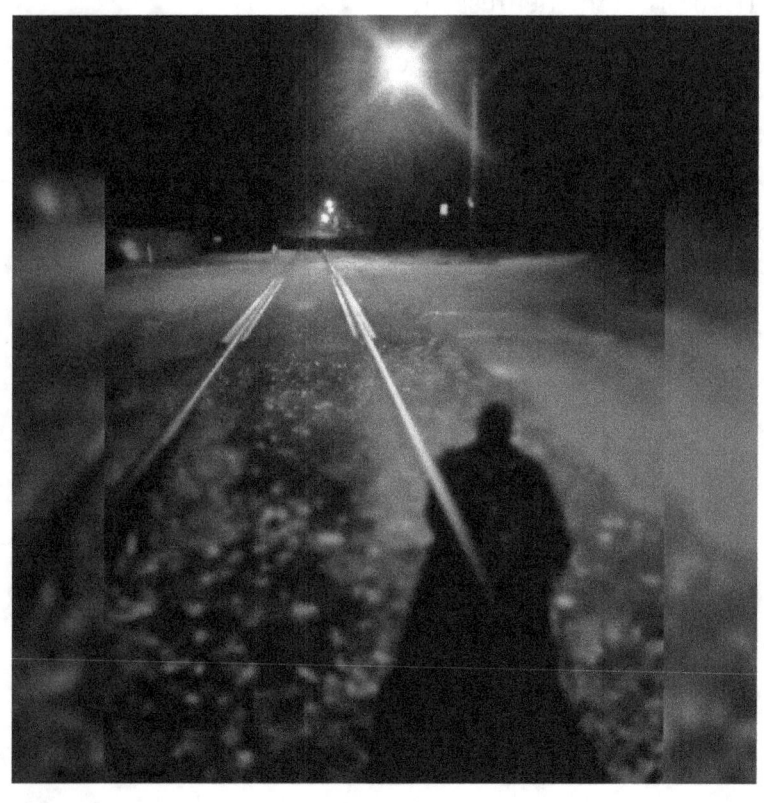

Cheap Realizations

Only costing chips off my soul.
Cheap realizations;
So cheap they're auctioned off.

To younglings in tattered clothes.
To offer some sort of spectacular spectacle,
And obscure reassurance,
To each, and every, insecurity they have.

To most,
Shadows and darkness seem daunting,
And scary; but to creatures of prey
It represents opportunity.

If I ever got the chance
To show you how much I cared,
I'd bleed through your fingers like

Wind through your hair.

I am all the people I've met.
The right people will smile at that,
The right people will cry.

Pack of Smokes

Walking through each keyhole,

We were feeling as we could.

Only in the best of ways.

But together the journey was like no other.

Fit for an obstacle course,

We climbed, traversed, laid, and rehearsed.

And like most things out of left field,

The feeling hit me like a stray 2 base pop up.

He was so sad, this man.

With a bag of empty beers

And a pocket full of dry, old, road cigarettes.

I was paying attention, sir, I swear it.

My left hand removed my pack,

My right clenched around hers,

But my focus was

Solely deciphering the camouflage you donned.

I lied a little bit, when I first spoke.

A clear indication I'm bad.

Matched with the dark clothes too big,

Tattoos, fitted hat, and white shoes.
I looked like trouble and lied like a pro.
Yes sir, to send you home with a pack of smokes.

Tunnel Vision

Through the longest hallway,
Your jaw reminds me
Of call centers.
Each person who called
Claimed a piece of us all.

There's no convincing,
Something's missing.
Entire parts have vanished;
Cities left stranded,
Abandoned and hissing.

Pissy drunk and fucked up
Off cocaine and lunch trucks,
And other things that lumped us
In the same category
Of people with sadder stories,
Have jumped up and stumped us.

Quite fine by lunch time;

My stomachs got lime

And not much shine.

I wish this feeling never died.

What about the parallels

And careful wells

Collecting all the rain in swells

To release in hell?

Colloquies all come free

And it's not just me.

There's an air of extreme;

Perfection is all just a dream.

Shiny and sheen.

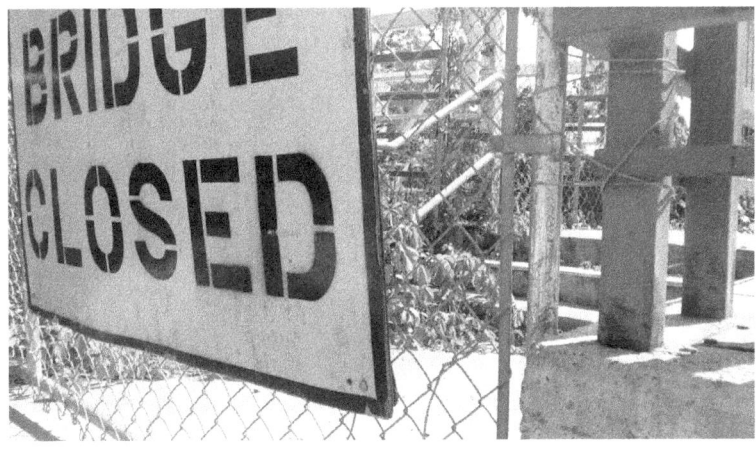

Travels Deep

I've been lacing these skates
To sail past the down state.
States of loss costs hurdles.
The earnest curdles
My hunger pains.
First, I was under pain,
Just a tad bit late.
Second, I know I
Can't escape it.
Can't re-tape it.
So, steadily I
Bind my time
To deconstruct,
And then reshape it.
But, that's me complacent?

Burrow that oil,
Save me those rich.

Because I'm hungry,

Yet, seasoned in switch.

And anything other than love

Gets treated like treason if

Everyone's pun

Is heated with

Devious thieves

Loading their guns.

And misleading their scene;

I'm almost over it.

The clover pits of a sober judge

Is almost blowing up

With no more lungs.

<u>Constituents</u>

I plead guilty to giving up;

It's never been enough.

You've all made me callous as fuck,

And it's all boiling up

Too much to care about my health.

I have no life,

So, I'm voracious in my chase of wealth.

In this dark environment,

I move through with stealth,

No one sees the pain.

I fight to live.

Every day, waiting for the pain to end.

I'm tired of moving forward

Only to defend.

The only reason I'm alive

Is the hope that one day

I can forget the dues I paid.

Feeling stressed and guilt ridden,
And seeing these looks of riddance,

I can see your true feelings
Hiding beneath your cold gazes,
Even the ones you keep hidden.

351

The crunch of the snow
Echoed upward
With hieroglyphs dancing
In every gust
My lungs painted in the sky.

Hear the metal slam of the door behind me.

Static played xylophones
Whose tunes require passwords.
Bitter cold only enhancing
The warm's trust,
I try to never look you in the eye.

Hear the metal slam of the door beside me.

Move things on the seat
So I can sit down.

Breathe in some cancer together,

And depart to our homes.

And you'd never know

After hearing that metal door slam behind me.

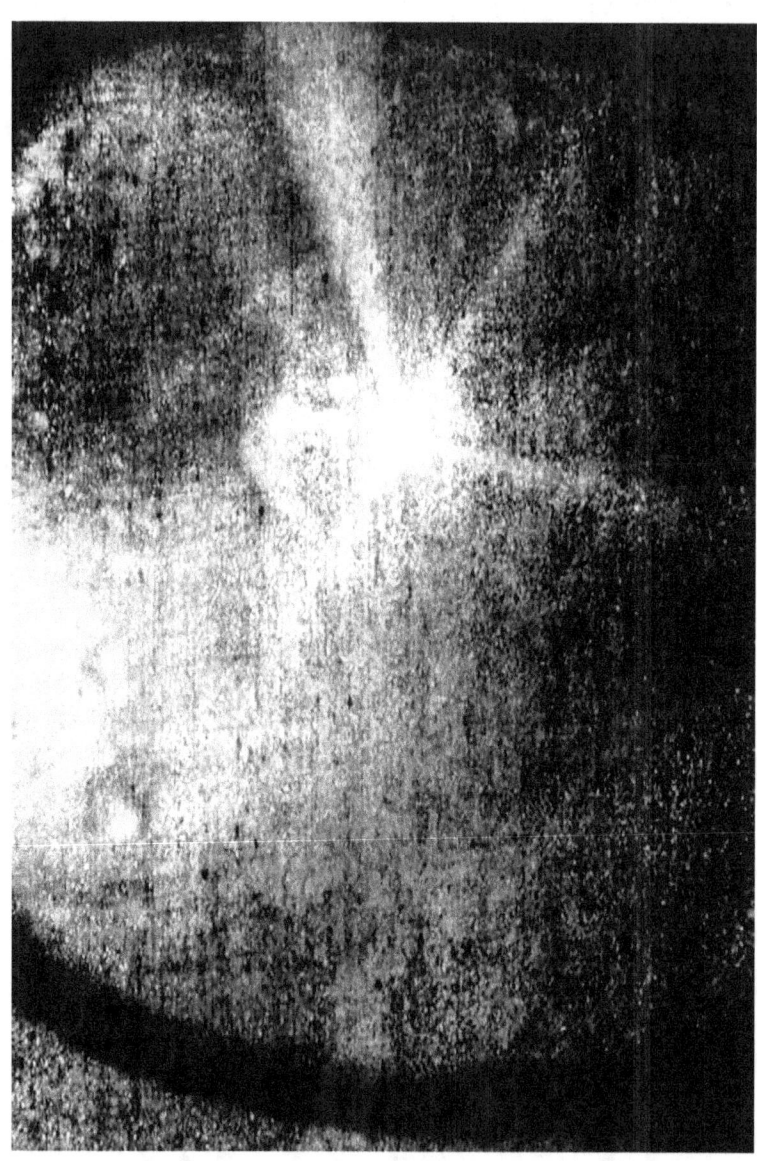

Windows

I can see you every day.

So close, I would hit you if I yawned.

But you're as equally transparent as apparent.

So, it dawned.

New ages to appease karma's inherent

Need to remind these thieves

The end has spawned.

I've adventured close to the surface,

And cremated most of my hope.

Those better days had a purpose

That wasn't watching you elope.

Much like writing in cursive,

Hand in hand, you're hurting me slow.

I'm scared to ask and find out If you had any clue.

I think I'd rather hide out

Than to see if you knew

That I sat in my cubicle's blind house;

Dreaming of you.

Seems I'm just high now.

But those ripples you sent me

Change in a spectrum of time.

I now know the words of "us and we",

And every other past line,

Were meant for you and he,

And I was nowhere in mind.

It teaches you

How important it can be

To know the true meaning of "I love you"

Is simply letting you be.

I could stand here and miss you,

Or be that tumbling leaf;

Scared and running away from you,

Ergo, making you miss me.

Perry Street

Intrigued like bees,
We will make honey.
You will see.

At the bar with a full drink,
You in that dress…
I can't think.

Cough out lines I practiced,
And like water in a mattress,
It made us both dense.

At home with my abandonment issues,
We climbcd a wall of abyss
And ended up sutured and stitched.

Since then, I've sent smokestacks
To get our tribe together once more

With all its dignity intact.

Save my sanity
Another morning, see you later;
Another later to abandon me.
Suck up my sorrows,
Stuff hopes into a sack.
It's either a gun, or tomorrow.

Little Stars

That speckle in the dim morning sky

Greeted my sightline as I walked out the door.

That little star, shining so bright

Against the invasive sun rising

To take it's light.

But that sparkle followed me.

Every minute in my peripherals

Glimmered remembrances of hope.

A hope that shows its face

As the ceiling light reflects atop my coffee,

Or dances across my cell screen;

Flickering on a moving pen,

Or shooting across the windows,

As cars zoomed to their dooms.

It made me feel warm.

Not in a UV sense, but in a knowing.

A knowing that there will be another flare

Shot into the deep purples.

Spinning around in circles,

I can see that hope is still thriving,

And leaving trails over previous spots

From staring into the sun for too long,

Almost changing their hue.

All the while,

I've just been thinking of you.

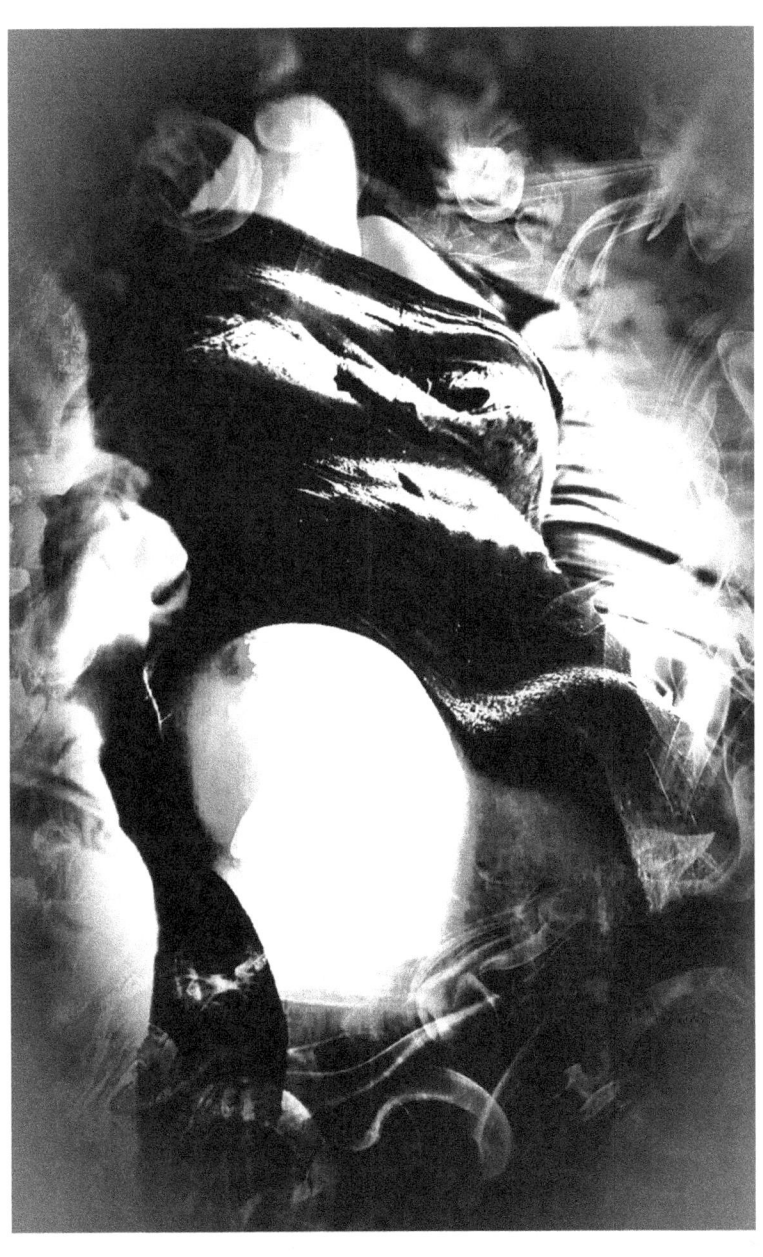

Pourer

The glimmer in your eyes
Caught mine across the bar.

Shining, lighting your aura;
Exploding like combusting stars.

The true meaning of star crossed,
We're like 50 shades of opposite.

Whirling around smiles,
Never concerning the cost.

For some reason, I couldn't resist;
A jar that the top doesn't fit.

Either not enough, or way too much,
And you can't keep the air in it.

I recall thinking of a time
Holding your soul in mine.

The heart you stole
As I write this alone.

" *'Jane, be still;*
Don't struggle so like a wild,
Frantic bird,
That is rending its own plumage

In its desperation.' **"**
–Charlotte Brontë

Acts of Those

Two books appeared on my doorstep today.

It was brisk, I and I, in my boxers.

Much like the sharp whiskey driven night searching

for something stronger to consume our brains.

There was no luck taming the artful screaming,

Or stop the introduction.

I wish life had Pandora installed and a next button.

Only if the Bolivians could kill me now would I die...

Not necessarily happy, but quick, at least.

And as the bright lights reminded me of a place

I'd never been,

I felt compelled with every drop of sin.

Thank you,

If you remember like I do.

Relevance

Hood on,

Sweeping through early morning dews with wet shoes,

I'm moving before the sun works up

Enough courage to break a shy dawn.

When the energy and I meet,

It knows not to ask me who I am,

For this vague and insatiable question

Irks my every cell.

My retort is always as simple as basic arithmetic,

And yet as deep as still water.

Me.

Where (M) is the multitude at which I exist.

(E) is everything I am, need, and love.

(C) the myth that is.

In this world $E=MC^2$ means:

I.

Am.

Relevant.

Undefined by the linear boundaries,

The societal bricklayers,

And copper pots.

Undiscovered by the masses;

Alone and fine with it.

A rarity in modern conformance.

Untraceable to those corrupted.

And, so unafraid that

I've grown unrelenting.

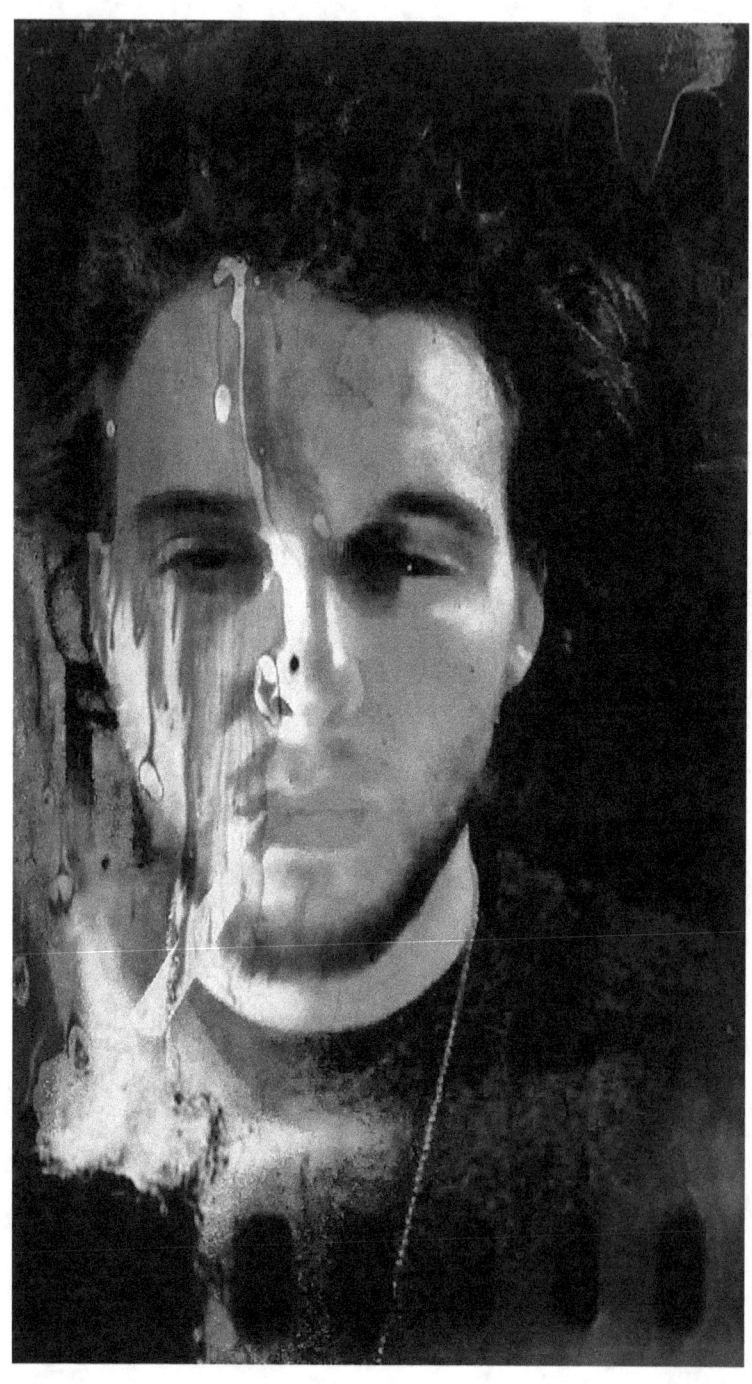

The Apple

Why do religions preach

That the love of money is the route of all evil,

Pass a plate, and ask for donations?

And, furthermore, if a wealthy man

Was affected that well from an organized religion,

Wouldn't they make sure

They're church survived forever?

No.

The rich have realized what we still have to;

The love of money

Is the route of all evil AND freedom.

Things like religion are merely forms of oppression

To keep us a level of servitude for our entire lives.

They warned us with the stories of Eve.

Live Graffiti

I woke up
After a day and a half,
With a billion-dollar idea.
My cocaine habit
Frowning I couldn't get
A gram and a half more.

No one will ever know,
But soon you'll see,
It was me.
It was me,
All along.

Twirls

Mornings flow into afternoon
In the most beautiful fashions
Wasting time could wear while I'm with you.

The lingering mist of your presence illuminates prisms

Through my life like streetlamps
Through the fog at 4am.

The sight of you cutting through
Compares not to the warmth I feel
With the air as still and calm as a lake.

As I walked in the adventure you became,
5, or 6, casual swirls and swells of the truth and static
Danced intermittently off the sharpest corners
Of my deepest worries
As if every last vapor of negativity

Was slowly, but stubbornly, swallowed and forgotten

By the positive atmosphere you solidified in my future.

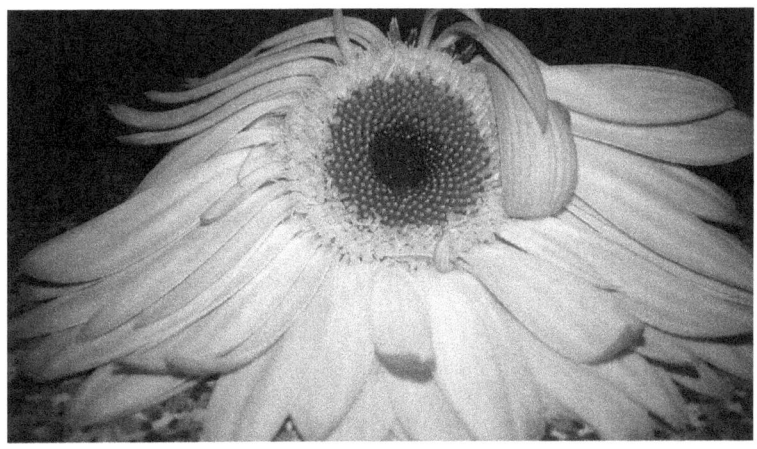

<u>Trips to the Moon</u>

Like the black sheep of his family,

He was unique and made his presence known,

Yet at the same time

Hated himself for what he'd become;

Apparently broken,

And inherently out-spoken.

It's not me; it's the waves I create.

It must be the drugs

In Assateague,

Budkushers and the Green Shop.

You have insufficient funds to send message.

But, my phone is good.

Like a diamond in the rough,

Our shine was formed underground, but…

Bitches don't drive Lincolns.

I lived a lifetime in the mouth of your vigor.

Dark places and dark spaces,

The only place I feel courageous.

I hate you all,

And I hope it's contagious.

Rescue me.

With Emergen-c, ibuprofen, orange juice,

Washcloth, soup, and sherbet.

A roof erases.

Beers and spliffs rise from the surface

Only to make *me* feel like *I'm* flying.

I remember the first joke I told in another language.

There were rolled up twenties,

And weirdly shaped papers,

Strewn throughout the dwelling.

Though, most of the money spent

Was funding a shady organization.

It should be sited,

It was not to be looked down upon in the right souls.

The current shit storm of my life

Rests completely on your shoulders,

And, it's funny that today

Was the first time I saw you...

Mostly because I haven't slept in my real bed

Since you last slept in it with me.

And you came the day I woke up in it

With somebody else.

You guys like me better on drugs,

And you'd probably have to say

Some pretty potent shit to get my mind back,

Because the best sex I've ever had without

psychedelics Was with a felon, Puerto Rican goddess.

I had to text myself today to remember

What it sounds like to receive one...

The stoves on,

But for really no reason.

Midnight writes are as wily as this whiskey

And as intoxicated as I.

Consumed, one could say;

They say,

He said and she said.

But your opinion doesn't matter;

Jameson told me sharply

And reminded me for 2 days after.

Feeling you pull away is like

Watching a child suffer through a telescope,

Your smile was the first one I saw today,

And I'll never forget it.

I thought as I left my laundry bag that maybe

You'd enjoy some coffee,

Decided it was too creepy,

And I was glad I didn't.

Especially when you walked back in

With exactly what I was going to get you.

This time last year I was preparing for Glassfestivities

By gargling a handful of mushrooms
Not yet dry enough.
Walking down the center of the street
Gives me flash backs from the chaos
Even as they set up.

It's not about what lies in wait,
But the waves you create
While you see how many drugs you can take.
Life's mistakes will soon fall short
Of a full birthday cake
While my nose is in a decanter
Smelling the decent shapes.

The love you feel from others
Is the love you'll always seek.

Sitting here,

Sitting here,

With my feet in the waves.

Each of these rays kiss my face as the tide rises.

Teasing my spine to my neck, and back down,

This fluid karma machine makes me drift to the

clouds.

The dream I had of that love till the end has ended...

What a way this ironic event has such a hold on me.

It's as if seeing that sunset silhouetting two hands.

Means nothing to the world,

But means the world to me.

Funny how small we are,

But, big we seem.

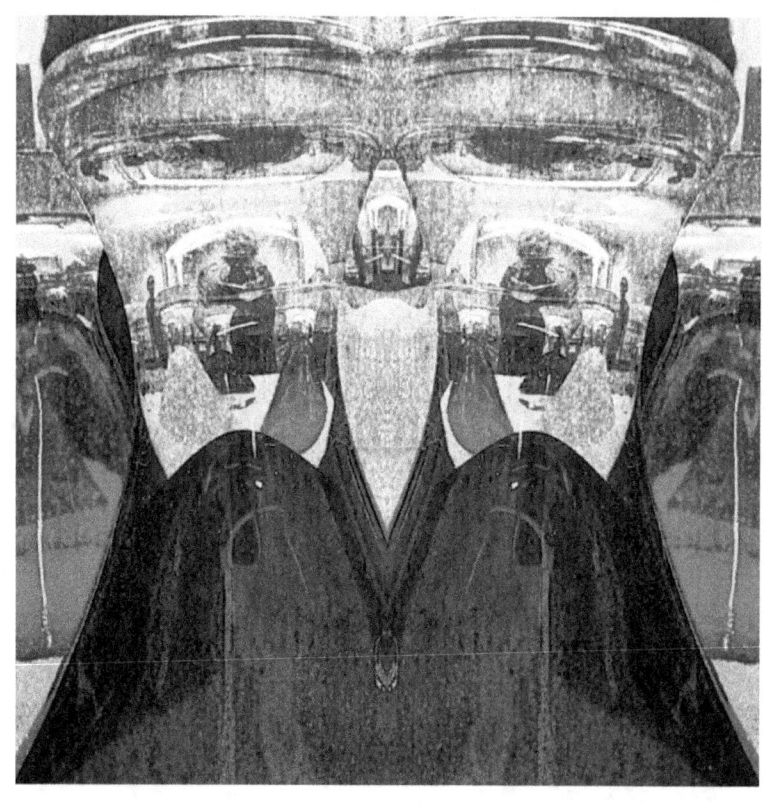

Pugilist

A porcelain Chipmunk,

With red eyes,

Watched every quarter sized spider

Rappel the shades,

Over the cliffs of vision,

And onto the sill;

Misty in essence,

And precipitous.

Evaporating downward,

Like a deity's hand

Wanted me to see

My worst fear

Trickle my sightline,

Hiding little drawn memories

Speckled across the grassy knolls

In my cortex.

Those tiny, little,

Red glows watched;

Their laughs bowing

Any structure I claimed

And clamored to cling to.

Bringing me back to when

Picnic tables and lawn chairs

Left their DNA under my nails.

Anymore and I, I could die.

Hence why I've never settled down.

How else do I explain I'm not allergic

To being subverted,

Only submissive?

And that what's good

For the exoskeleton

Is bad for the endocrine?

Maybe a doctrine of self

Will seemingly show

Sanity's silky thread

Is sadly strewn,

But excessive

In being

Resilient.

Commonly

The guided road to freedom is
Littered with near sighted bots
Setting up obstacles to forbid your smiling.
Disparity will well up and fall like ice drops of hope
That sizzle in the coals burning
Throughout my sight of the city.
It's damning.

The introverted perception feels the pain
Of what was done to them
And projects how they were treated
Back into the world
Through thoughts of empathy and covalence.
Only to be completely met at a standstill,
A balance beam of "equal weights";
The cowardice of wanting peace
Confronts the cowardice of needing control.
The cowardice of not needing a leader
Has come to face the cowardice of power.

Smoke swirls in and out of the lights
Projected by fireflies of past lives
Thrown up in the sky
By the very people taking it away;
As the ants of this empire,
The builders of this Atlantis,
Move to drown the baby

Freedom failed to create.

I see all this like a child grasps a snow globe.
Watching, mesmerized, insurmountable freedoms
Flying by our heads as we stand in the middle
Of our contained security net.
When it all settles, we will realize our freedom
No longer flies;
Shaking the safety of the outer globe
Is the only chance for fresh air,
Like waves of guerrilla warfare for negativity.
Feed it to me with a fury,
Instead of being the person who can't.

Who would've thought?

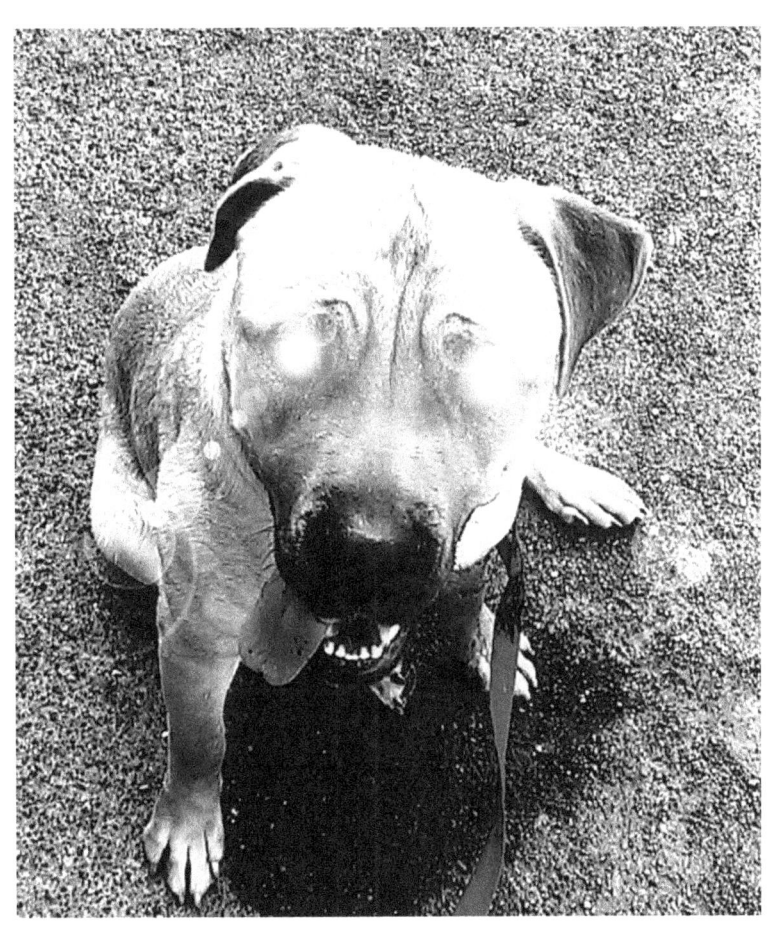

Roars and Ohms

Treat things like Buddha,
Run things like Che.

When you learn
That everyone and everything else
Is out for themselves,
You learn
Self-reliance.

When you figure out
That's how anybody and anything
Became great,
You not only become truly free,
You become the strongest
You will ever be.

Eight

I set foot today in a new location.

I tried to jump and see how much more

Hang-time I'd gained.

And when I landed every face around me

Made my whole demeanor crawl,

As if cold water pierced the tips of my toes,

Back into the room with the wallflowers.

Maybe, if we get the recipe right,

I can bloom again,

Like the water was warm and our gravity

Brought back the tide.

Bloom again like a nightshade

To put my own brand of poison,

Labeled as fun with three x's,

Out to experience something else new,

Alive,

And unholy.

Then after hearing the riverbed slowly wake me,

As gently as mother never did,

I stood up with a gaze of begrudging happiness.

Pain seeks to satisfy my old rocking chair,

Yet I have to continue its rocking.

And, maybe, that's a sign.

A Big neon sign reading, "I was in the right place;

That room with the wallflowers."

Maybe, in hindsight,

It never even fucking mattered,

But, we got the recipe right.

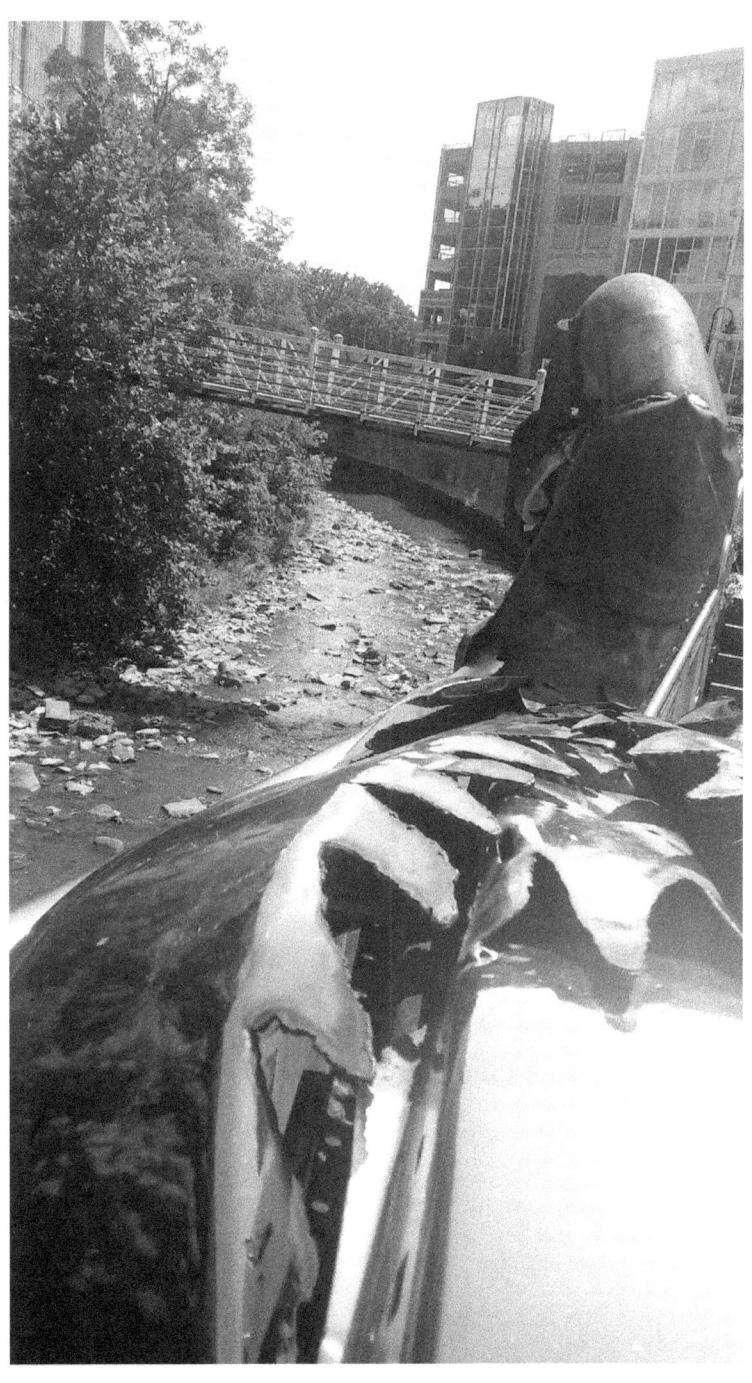

Noose

Cheers;
Here's to the completely superfluous
Notch on my belt you've become.
Much against my wants.

Too bad you couldn't foresee your own
Future night terrors.
But maybe that's the thing about
An open-minded introspection.

It's not the loop,
Nor the belts dagger,
But the jeans that gives the belt
Purpose to come together.

Battery Trick

I have to text Frank today
    About the trick with the battery.

Yesterday, I never could've invented today,
    Until I saw today re-invent yesterday.

Black Sheep

Having confidence in what you're doing,
And where you are going,
Is essential to never
Having a goal too far.

Knowing what you're worth,
And being comfortable and unmovable
In every stance you take,
Will make sure the life you want
Is the life you have.

Red Tailed Hawk in the Back Seat

I was wondering,
Asking if today was worth getting out of bed.
The Beast wanted the bathroom and needed to eat.

Hunger wasn't the only demon roaring its ugly head,
With 4 of us packed in a small car,
Almost a circus of sorts.
The powder kicked up by wheels turning too fast
Went right up my nose
After it napped on a phone's screen.
Big glasses filled with everything else we needed
Made smoke almost come out of our ears
As the madman and we
Descended to lower parts
Of the highest part
Of the state and country.

Friends.
Oh, friends we all are in the name
Of one thing, and one thing only.
Fun.
Chaos.
Any synonym that fits, really.

Each of the exits blew by
Like the rows and rows of trees
We went through.

As we still inched closer
Red Tailed Hawks exploded
Out of every on ramp we took;
Spreading their wings bald eagle
While I watched from the backseat;
Still not where we should be.

Drums.
Drums I hear on the horizon
Make war sounds we have been dancing to
For 27 years, and even harder to today,
Even though, we had to.
Beautiful art exhibits for the imaginary fairies
And spirits perpetuated the war drums
And only got prettier.
Maybe it was substances I waped in the wipe,
But chills of freedom ran through
Each and every nerve ending.

Dancing.
Dancing in circles,
We all smiled.

Ponds and pollywogs made sure of that.
Nobody judges the skunk's cloud or laughter,
Just chased their next bottles of wine
With photographs of paradise and lost trails.
This cryptic Eden spoke ear-shattering joys
Of living the life for a few hours
Until all of us rejects were needed
Back in formation at once.
I don't actually know if anyone was ready
To operate heavy machinery,

But, each iron gate swung open
To let us all fly.

Jamming.
Jamming,
We all grew weary of having to see
The same old sight, and sang
Until the neighbors could tell we were on one.
Going back seemed all too important
For our friendships to last
With each tidal of life that hit.

Opening the door, the Beast ran out of her room
And promptly asked for love,
Relief, and replenishment.
I had so much fun
I asked if it was worth getting back in bed.

I was wondering.

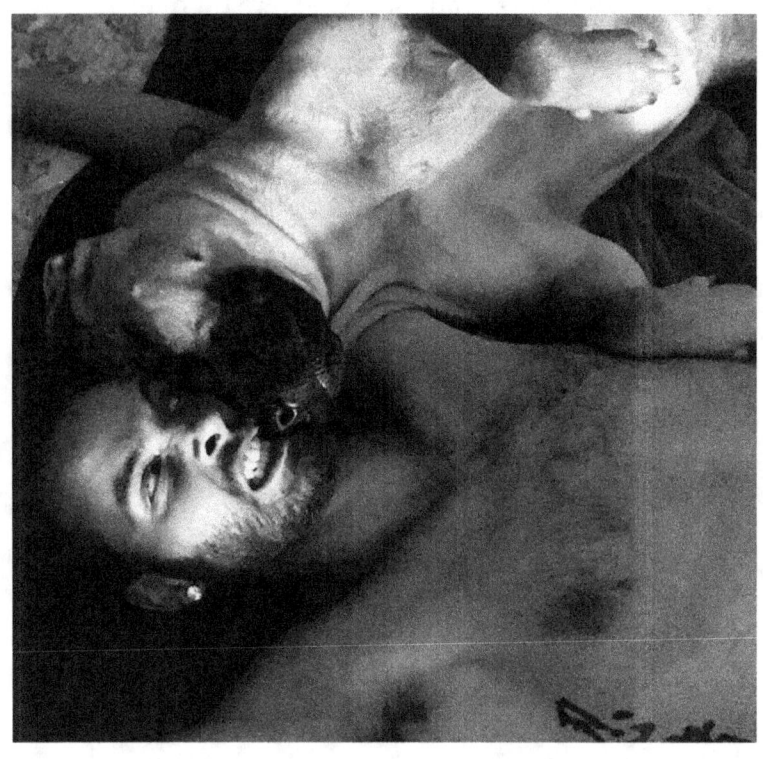

Smudge

Windows smudge under the grease of these paws
Pressed slightly too hard.
The smudges covered the squares
Lining the glass with teeth,
Devouring every sense of hope that was left
In abundance.

Walking back and forth between wants and laws,
Reminds me this isn't who we are.
Each and every streak noticed raged deep within me,
Inciting every bit of exhausted incepts
In redundancy.

I can't.
I can't.

Roped with a rock from the past
Has never kept me in one spot.

Let go of the rope and, in turn, me too.

Holding onto me

Is only limiting your own agenda.

One hand covering your eyes fast

Won't save you from hearing my plot;

One I devised specifically for you.

Walk right past that tree

With all those branches to mend us.

I can't.

I can't.

Computer desks aren't the reality,

Nor is your Buddha.

Killing him will only free you

In the eyes of every passerby,

Smudges, streaks, and all.

Ask the windows with teeth,

Or the ghost of prolusion.

With no company left to bill you,

There are no personal ads in the classifieds,
Full of freaks.

I can't.
I can't.

I can't be free watching you all stay imprisoned,
Or seeing followers in the crowd.
I can't follow along,
Like the smudges,
The narrative venture makes me cringe.

Latch your claws into never fearing decisions,
Or constantly thinking out loud.

I can sing a song.
Like the smudges,
Your streak free windows make me cringe.

I can.

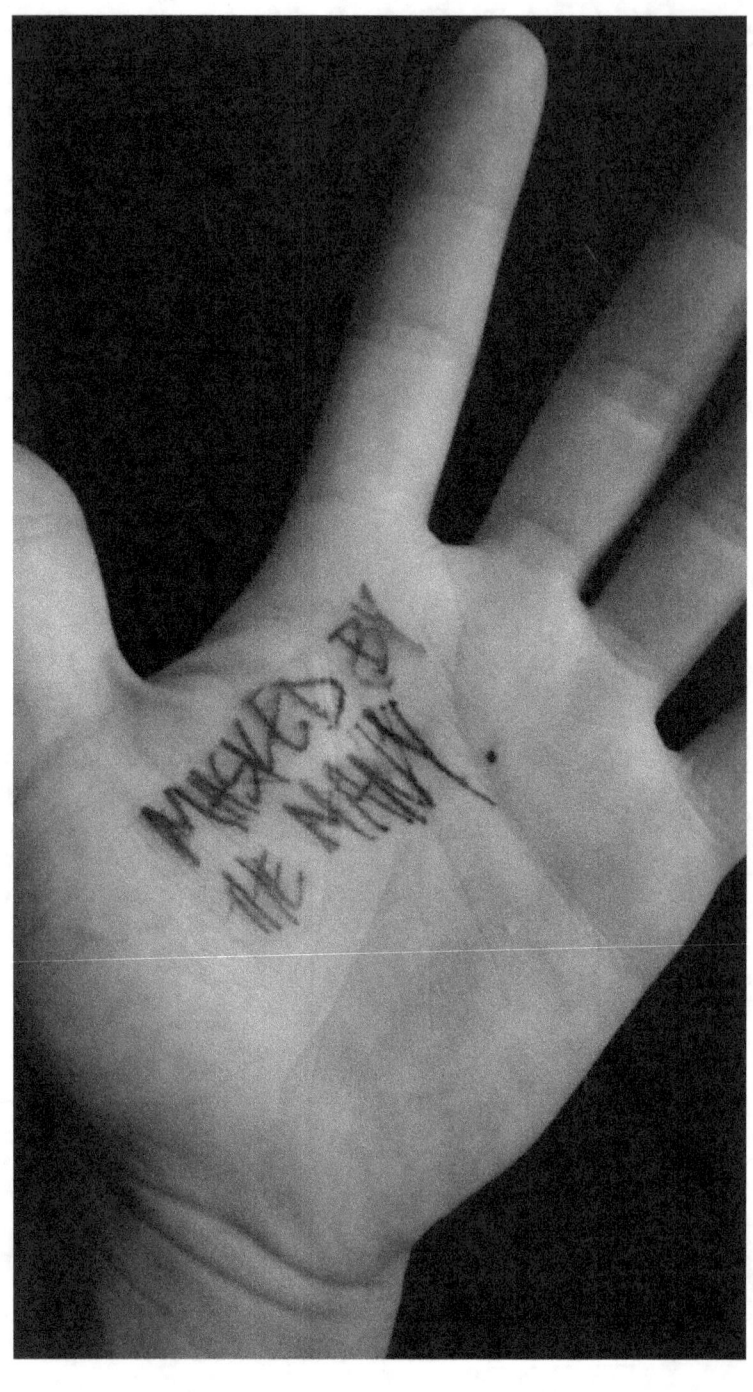

Bad Advice

In a world where chaos comes

Unseen and unapologetically,

Roll it.

Smoke it.

Take it on the chin and keep moving.

Appreciate every unique situation

And the universally charming little comedy

Life hands out like the doll during the depression.

Furthermore;

Dig deeper.

Experiment.

Explore.

Invent

And recycle.

Every moment is a lesson to be learned,

Each lesson usually boils down

To staying true to yourself.

And when you do things out of an unknown urge,

It's not a disorder.

It's an innate need

To be

Free And happy.

Fuck everyone.

Leaf Poem Part 2

I'm the first leaf of the fallen...

Not saddened by being alone,

Looking back at everyone hanging out

On the tree still;

Laughing and wiggling at how different he is.

Not fully understanding

He is free.

Cold Costs

Green windows and seventeen hints

Lost in productivity.

An answer slowly dances by,

But the condensation keeps me fogged in;

Locked in the moisture my independence craves.

Craving like the man on a corner

Waiting for me to pass by.

And, even though I can smell his plan

Because it's thick with tension,

Not to mention the pot

With water not yet hot enough

To boil my stubborn ass,

Must you ask why?

The only two choices you left me with:

Lose my life, or my life savings;

I'm a few bucks short of a fuck

About the lazy God that won't quite save me.

Luckily, I'm crazy.

I abandon sights and open life,

Make my own lane,

And drain your plight.

I'm dangerous like a cryptogram

With symbols you've never had experience with.

Strange lefts and rights,

Dots and what-nots.

Cues, longs, shorts, hues and knots.

It's brain numbing,

And I plan on treating every dying brain cell

Like a falling supernova;

Decaying to revitalize more life

Into an ever-expanding universe.

Ready to give love a chance for hope,

Because back in our reality

It hasn't been organic,

Just based off our salaries

Until we turn to ghosts.

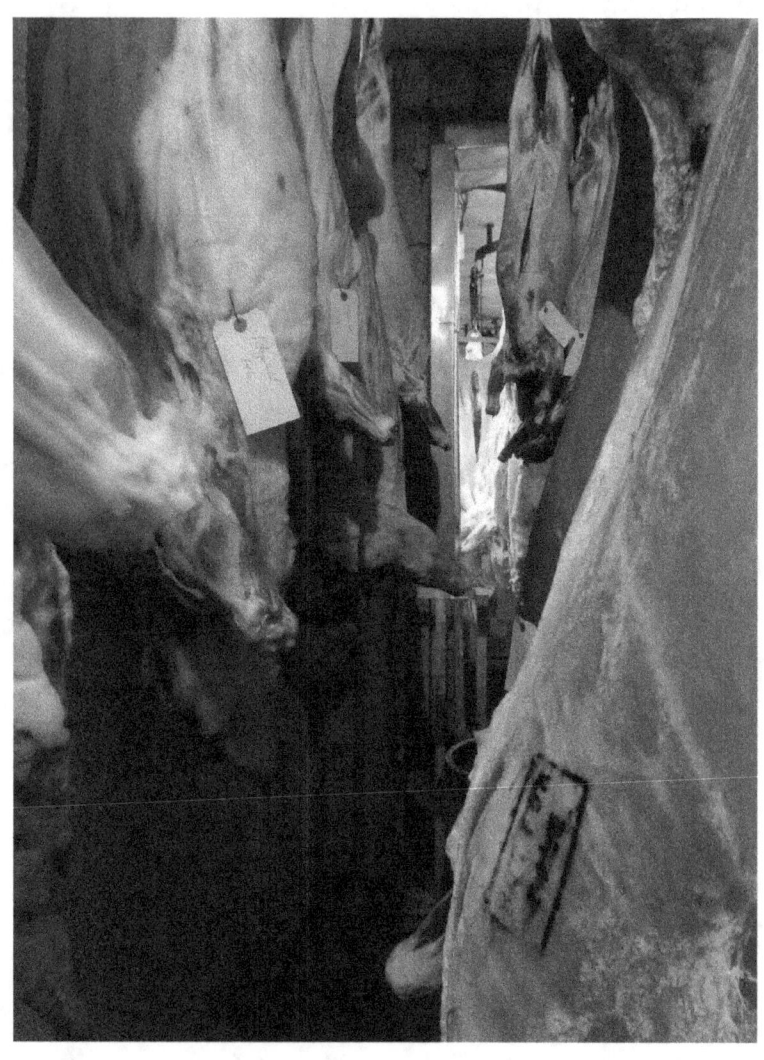

The Guy I Saw Was Clean Shaven...

Aug. 18th, 2015.

2:45 A.M. EST.

My beard just saved my life.

I'm never shaving this thing again.

Pursuit

Those who choose

To let the problems

Of the world

Bother them

Will never know

How good it feels

To wake up

Smiling

Everyday

For no reason

Other than being alive.

Ancient Riddles

As I walk by these
Frustrating bad dreams,
My eyes stay fixed
Like beams
On the prize.

I've sought like a river after your ocean.
Danced around your boulders

And slivers alike with effortless motion.
Parkour via nature's strength.

I'll make me happy now
With the same tenacity as your bow.

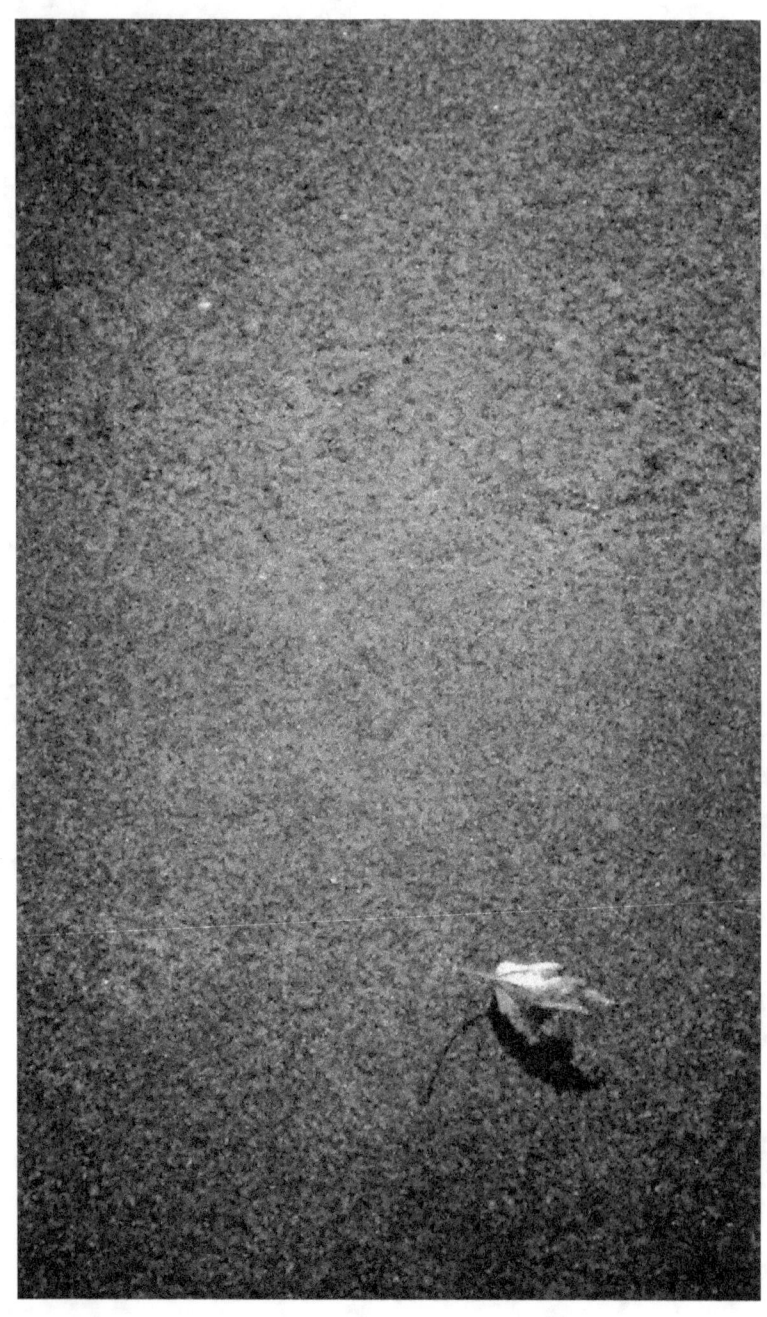

More Bad Advice

Inspire chaos to work in your favor.

Calls from the Requiem

It made more sense before,

But there's currently a famine of love

For Chihuahuas in Philadelphia,

And it's becoming an epidemic.

I feel more lured to the waves of uncertainty.

Those enticing waves.

Moments of Rebellion

With my Adidas' finally on the pavement,

And my hood finally shadowing my face,

A small little snowflake lands on my nose.

As oddly quiet as tonight could be,

I could almost hear it melt.

Soliloquies of Kendrick vibrates everything,

Inordinately shaking the peripheral red light.

Business was at hand like a doctor's medicine bag,

And my socks were completely soaked through.

I couldn't blame everyone for being agoraphobics.

And surely the Beast's nose was pressed, too.

But there was nothing going to stop me,

Or hinder my insatiability or strife,

Especially another synchronized red light.

Parks and venues were closed,

Turning even fun places into bedeviled smoke spots;

My jacket was camouflaged by the snow.

And unvarying winds were fighting against me,

Bludgeoning my steps to an almost ceasefire.

Mechanically, I creaked and almost ticked, Right

before the changing red light.

Shaking off the retired snowbirds like friends,

I was indebted to the warmth inside.

I could hear whines of contention from Beast

Wanting out of her room with me.

The movie I left playing had all but stopped.

It never really made sense to me,

But nothing ever really did at red lights.

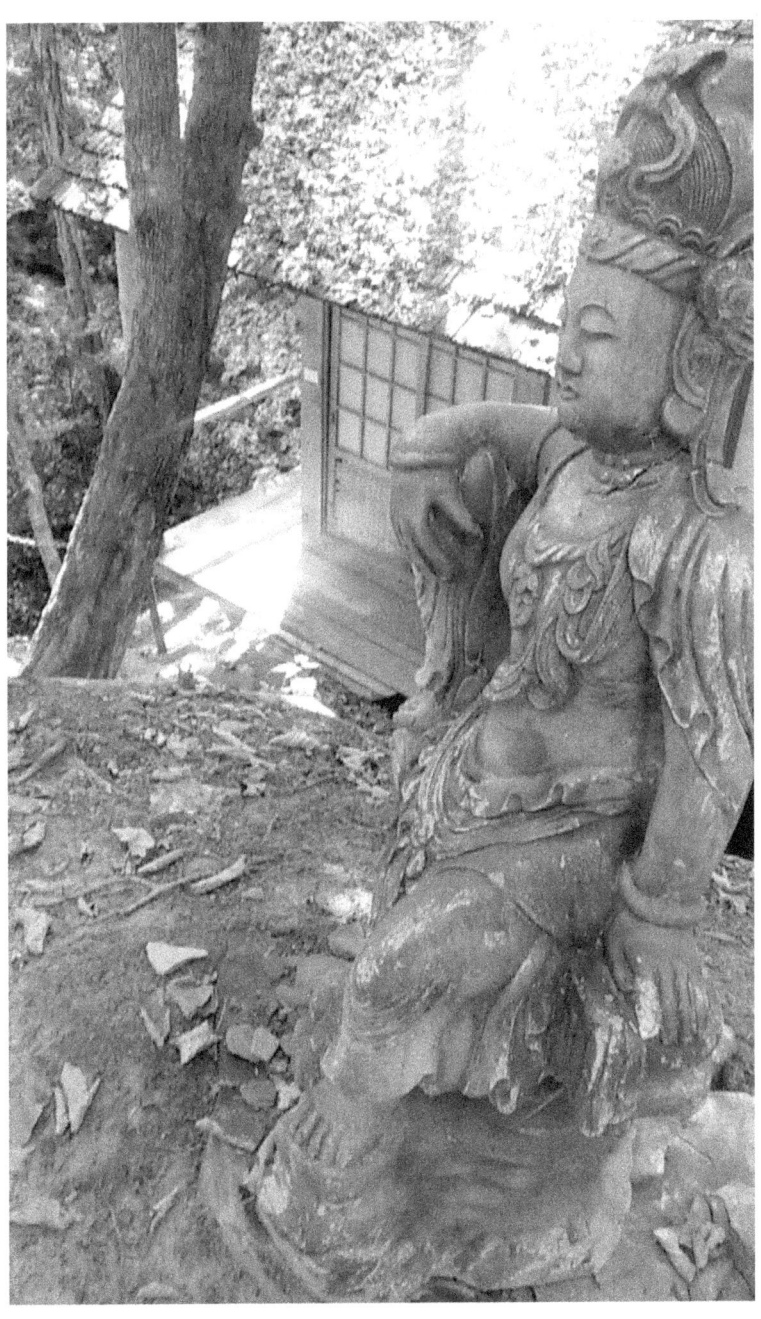

Commanding the Past
into a Projection of Future

Love is life in sheep's clothing,

Where animosity drives herds

Of sleep by waves we've never heard.

Far from gravity, it can be done.

It can be done in

Room 71, which has two of the same paintings

Staring at obituaries I wrote about strangers.

Those twin paints twirled in chairs all day

Until they were done.

Until they were done with

Golden hands, from

Loped off dangers;

Shielding the shade with sunlight,

And a hunger that growled at co-inhabitants
Begging to be in.

Begging to be in when

Clicks and clangs
Sloughed under water.
Even animals scattered
To a place in 8th grade
When you couldn't bring food downstairs
Until you were done.

Until you were done with

The kids that said they saw a robber.
A few and far between
Can even dream of the sighs
An owl must take
Before her lungs are done.

Before her lungs are done

Up in pretty dresses for sachets;

Telling tall tales around

The punch bowl, as

Uneven as the vertigo,

Later when life was done

When life was done for

3 hours of the day at a time,

And the Captain's log

Ends with "Where was I going?"

Only the vessels are never found

When the tide is done.

When the tide is done at

This time in the afternoon,

When even sharks look like lunch;

In a harbored feeling of Identified Patient Syndrome,

A psychologist said, "When we are done".

When we are done

We huddled together in laughter and drunkenly

Swayed in a palm's trance

That traced my palm

Back to civilization might never happen

Until I am done.

I am done.

BANG! *BANG! BANG!*

Yugo's eyes bolted open and Beast was already alerted at the door. After everything that has happened the past few months, there's only one person that it could be.

BANG! BANG!

The door started rattling and it sounded as if someone was trying unnaturally hard to pick the lock. Coming in here wasn't smart for whomever it was with Beast roaming about. She was friendly with me since I saved her, but only me. Especially after that rude awakening, it just wouldn't be smart.

More rattling and shaking, then *BAM! BAM BAM! BAM!* It sounded as if someone was kicking the door now.

Yugo got up as quietly as he could and grabbed the loaded 12 gauge he kept in the corner as the person moved to the window to try to pick that lock. Yugo laughed once he realized he couldn't get it open. The "2" bedroom was more like a cramped 1 bedroom with a large closet that Yugo used to keep Beast in when he was working. Now that he wasn't working, he just used it for storage.

Moving on, the person went to try the back porch that Yugo had preemptively had stacked bags of garbage and cans on to block off.

It was quiet for about 3 minutes and Yugo heard him come back to the front door again.

BANG! BAM! BANG BANG! BAM!

He was getting more violent with every time at the door, not to mention more pathetic at attempts of locksmithing. He tried the second front door, which was equally as blocked off of as the back porch with a bike, air conditioner, road salt, and random tools in a small hallway. The person ransacked through the blockade and still tried to pull open the latched door. Yugo just stood quietly with the shotgun aimed steadily at whatever door he went to, and Beast ready directly on the opposite side. The person knew that she was in there, and the gun, but was still acting like a lunatic. Yugo came to terms with the fact he was going to have to shoot someone; a feat he tried to avoid his entire life. He just realized that the man on the other side of the door had malice intent planned for when he trampled through whatever entrance he could.

After the forty-minute onslaught that won the award for "Worst Alarm Clock in the World", the person finally got tired of trying and it sounded as if he'd left. Yugo had spent 2 years in Harlem every weekend, roaming about at three and four in the morning, the only white boy around for a mile in either

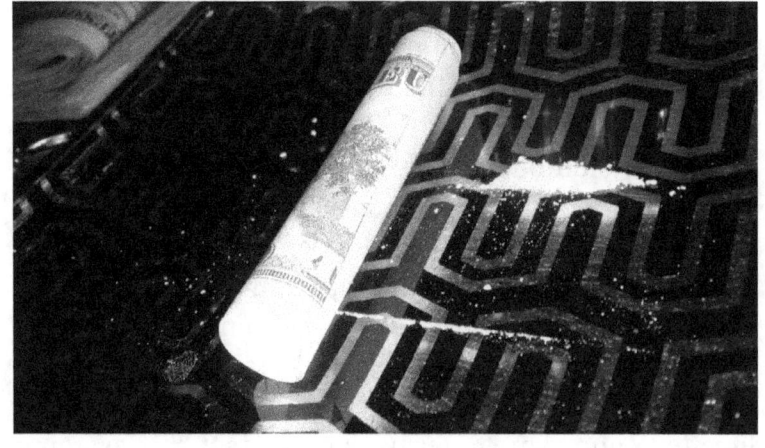

direction. He learned early on to spot traps and had innate street smarts… Part of how he ended up there in the first place. So, Yugo waited.

Yugo moved to Beast's room and peered through a sliver in the Grateful Dead drapes. He saw the person sitting in his truck and not moving. He watched the man in the black Dodge for about fifteen minutes, standing surgically solemn. Once the pickup started to pull away, Yugo sighed and started to shake. He had stayed out of trouble for so long now, and done so well in life, regardless of losing everything the month prior after Murphy decided to take a shit on his life, and just narrowly escaped prison, again.

He shook for about an hour and decided to plan his escape until the adrenaline left his system. A beach, beautiful weather and women, great drugs and jobs… How could he not? By the end of October, he would be gone without ever looking back.

"…Only live your life as it is, not bound to anything."
-Siddhartha Gautama

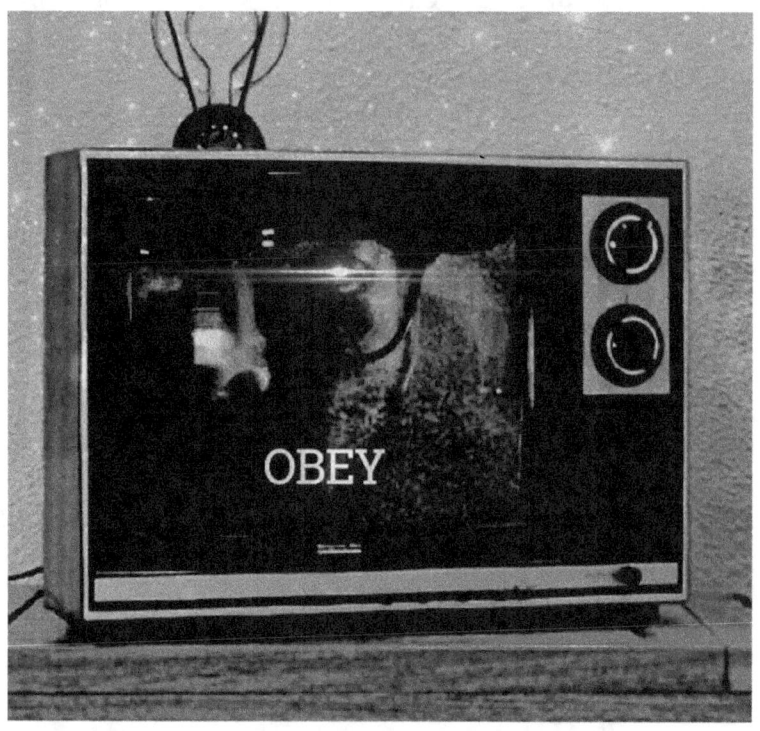

www.ingramcontent.com/pod-product-compliance
Lightning Source LLC
Chambersburg PA
CBHW070335220526
45467CB00001B/140